AN INTRODUCTION TO VEDIC ASTROLOGY

SPIRITUAL SCIENCE OF THE ANCIENTS

by

HOWARD BECKMAN

Any copy of this book issued by the publisher as a paperback is sold subject to the condition that it shall not by way of trade or otherwise be lent, resold, hired out or otherwise circulated, without the publisher's prior consent, in any form of binding or cover other than that in which it is published and without a similar condition including these words being imposed on a subsequent purchaser.

© 1994 Howard Beckman

Balaji Publishing Co.

First paperback edition 1995

All rights reserved. No part of this publication may be reproduced or transmitted in any form or by any means, electronic or mechanical, including photocopy, recording, or any information storage and retrieval system, without permission in writing from the publisher.

ISBN 0 9525172 0 5

Printed and Bound in Great Britain
by
Vision Printers
Tel: 0171 281 6369

Dedication

I dedicate this work to my spiritual master His Divine Grace A.C. Bhaktivedanta Swami Prabhupada who has forced my eyes open from the darkness of ignorance with the torchlight of knowledge. It is only out of his love and compassion upon this poor soul that I have been able to gain the slightest understanding of vedic knowledge, the ultimate aim of which is love of God. I offer my prostrate obeisances eternally at his lotus feet.

I wish to thank Mike Wright of the Isle of Wight for his incredible expertise in editing this book, done with his usual keen sense of precision, and Gina Wright for her patience and encouragement during the tedium of his efforts. Special thanks to Jennifer Keelan for her many hours of work on the computer entering all Mike's changes, her encouragement without which this book may never have been written, and most of all for her selfless love and devotion to me throughout.

TABLE OF CONTENTS

Page No.

Introduction i

Part 1,
Vedic Astrology: Your Personal Roadmap To Success 1
Physical Health 3
Mental, Emotional and Spiritual Health 9
Relationship Compatibility Using Astrology 15
Human Sexuality 19
Discovering Your Potential and Choosing a Career 21
Prosperity and Positive Thinking-Does it Really Work? 23
Consciousness and Spirituality 25
Practicality Of Astrology 29
Summary Points of Part 1 31

Part 2,
Understanding The Horoscope 35
The Planets, Signs and Houses 37
Planets in the Signs and Houses 49
The Stars 79
Temporary Natures of Planets 87
Rulership (Lordship) Yogas 89
Interpretation of the Chart and Predicting the Future 113
Planetary Aspects 119
Main Points From Part 2 119

Part 3,
Remedial Measures, Successful Progress and Conclusion ... 121
Remedial Measures in Astrology 122
Gemstone Therapy 123
The Seven Secrets of Successful Progress 127
Sample Horoscope 130
Conclusion 133

INTRODUCTION

Today there is a resurgence of interest in the West towards the spiritual sciences, of which vedic, or Indian, astrology is most prominent. Unfortunately, astrology is mostly misunderstood in the West, viewed as a purely esoteric science, without a basis of scientific understanding. This is a grave misconception, yet it is understandable considering the degradation to which it has been subjected.

Many people have little, or no, true knowledge of this great and holy science, thinking it to be, for the most part, in the realm of fantasy. Even those who have attempted to delve into it have been frustrated by the unfamiliar terminology and concepts on the subject. This is because most such books are written for those that wish to learn how to actually cast horoscopes, rather than simply as an aid to understanding a chart.

I am writing this book to hopefully fill such a gap for those that wish a simple and concise text to help them understand the purpose of the astrological science, as well as a handbook to understanding your own horoscope.

There will be no instructions on how to cast a horoscope. There are many texts delineating the mathematics for doing so and a selection can be found at any bookstore, although in this modern age the vast majority of astrologers use computers to cast the horoscopic charts. This book is meant for those that have their chart done by a vedic astrologer and wish to further understand it, as well as those that want to learn the usefulness of astrology in general.

The main reason that many have little respect for astrology in the West is simply due to lack of knowledge. It is thought of as simply a means of fortune-telling, which is far from the truth. There are many unscrupulous people who have but a little knowledge of this science, yet profess to be bona-fide astrologers, taking advantage of the ignorance of the general populace in this regard. The type of astrology based on Western sun signs, as found in most newspapers and many magazines, is, for the most part, useless. It is considered to be for entertainment purposes only and is not taken seriously due to the extremely general nature of it's supposed predictions for those born during the time the sun is in a particular sign. It has given a "black-eye" to the science, in the minds of many. This is a great shame for the true bona-fide science of astrology is meant to enlighten human society.

Vedic astrology is not only extremely accurate in helping an individual to understand what his or her future will be during this lifetime, but gives an understanding as to the true nature of matter and spirit, allowing knowledge to be gained of who we are and how to achieve success on all levels..... physical, mental or emotional and spiritual. A correct horoscope may be likened to a good road map for travelling between two distant cities. Using a detailed map, proper care can be taken to avoid danger. If the map shows a narrow road through mountains with dangerous curves and embankments, then any sane person will go slowly, keeping their eyes fixed carefully on the road and hands tightly on the wheel. If it shows the road to be wide and straight, with little in the way of obstacles, it is possible to go faster and be more relaxed on the journey. An accurate horoscope may be used as a road map on life's journey. At times of difficulty, or when negative karma is destined to manifest itself, you should take care. To take risks at such times, physically, financially, or otherwise is like speeding around mountain passes at night, where it is easy to have a major accident, incurring major losses in one way or another. At times, when you know the cards are "stacked in your favour", that is the time to pull out the stops and go all out to achieve success.

To begin with we need to understand what the science of astrology is. An astrologer does a horoscope which shows a map of the heavens at the time of birth. The different planets are shown at the exact place they were situated, in a particular zodiacal sign, at the moment you were born. Many people are familiar with the sun's movements, as when you look in your newspaper at the astrology column it shows the dates of the sun's passing through the various signs of the zodiac. The sun takes one full year to pass through all the signs. That is what it means when a person in the West says, "I'm a Taurus", or "I'm a Leo". It means that at the time they were born the sun was in Taurus, or Leo.

The zodiac is an imaginary sphere including the heavens. Within this sphere, all of the planets, including the sun and moon, are travelling in their respective orbits. It is divided into twelve equal parts of thirty degrees each which are the signs of the zodiac. Originally these signs corresponded to fixed constellations of stars, but due to the procession of the equinox (moving at approximately 50.25 seconds a year) this correlation is nonexistent at present. Therefore, after many years of this discrepancy there is about a twenty three degree difference between the constellations and signs of the same names. That is why someone who had always thought their sun was at fifteen degrees Leo would discover that, according to the eastern system, the sun would have been at 22 degrees Cancer. The Eastern system is called the sidereal zodiac and the Western called the tropical zodiac. Although the Western system is quite useful, having proved itself to be such for personality traits, especially the Eastern system is far more accurate for predictive astrology. The Eastern system also teaches the uses of remedial measures to strengthen a horoscope, as in gem therapy, whereas the Western system has no such system of self- help to strengthen weaknesses or to counteract negative influences in the horoscope.

To only consider the sun sign is a very incomplete picture as all the planets are in signs of the zodiac, and their positions at the time of birth are just as important as the position of the sun. Since the planets represent different things we must know where they all were, to gain a complete picture.

There are twelve "signs", illustrating different natures or qualities of the energies represented by the planets.

Then there are the twelve "houses", which represent the different applications or categories of life. For instance the moon represents the mind and an individual, with the moon in Leo, will have a powerful mind, as the qualities of Leo are strong and fiery. Depending on which house it is situated in will determine different attributes relating to different areas of life, such as health, wealth, career, happiness, relationships with others, nature of the personality, etc.

The way we know which sign goes in which house is according to the rising sign, or ascendant. Whatever sign was due east on the horizon at the time of birth is the rising sign. This sign is placed in the first house and all the other eleven signs follow in their natural order. Therefore, if Leo is rising at the time of birth, then it is put in the first house, Virgo in the second, Libra in the third, Scorpio in the fourth, Sagittarius in the fifth and so on.

Gaining an understanding of the effects of having a particular planet in a certain sign in a certain house will help you to understand this life and beyond. I say beyond, because this science is not meant simply for understanding this present lifetime but for understanding the bigger picture.

We are not these bodies, rather our eternal nature is "spirit", unending, and unchanging in nature. It is only due to the covering of the body that we identify so much with this world and it is only our bodies which are subject to birth, death, old age and disease. At the time of death, or leaving the body, the spirit soul leaves and goes on to another situation determined by the "karma" (results of actions performed) created while in the present body.

The science of astrology is based on the science of "transmigration of the soul". This is the journey of the spirit soul from body to body, in lifetime after lifetime, due to karma, or the reactions to the actions performed in life. Therefore, when we read a chart, we are understanding the quality of the activities performed in the former life. According to our actions we are awarded a particular type of body in which to enjoy, or suffer, within this world. Anyone that has had their horoscope done by a qualified astrologer must accept this principle. How else are we able to reveal a life, past, present and future, including the nature and machinations of the mind and innermost feelings? It is not due to being psychic, although a developed "sixth sense" is necessary, but a very real and scientific method of "reading" the chart.

Since proper practice of this science requires great intellect, as well as "clarity of perception," take care to find an astrologer who lives by the "superior" principles of life. "Superior" principles means spiritual principles, for an astrologer who has not attained a level of greater physical, mental, and spiritual health cannot help others to do so. A person should not take the title astrologer after only reading a few books and learning the mechanics of the science. It takes adherence to higher spiritual principles of life to gain the necessary intuition to be able to help others. You wouldn't choose an attorney who is lazy and therefore unwilling to do the proper research on behalf of your case, nor choose a doctor who is 150 pounds overweight and chain-smokes cigarettes, nor an accountant whose clients are often called upon for a financial audit by the taxation department. Take just as much care in choosing an astrologer. A qualified vedic astrologer is also qualified as a spiritual guide, career counsellor, psychologist, marriage or relationship counsellor and capable of diagnosing likely physical weaknesses and ailments in the body. To illustrate this last category, up until a few hundred years or so ago, doctors were required to also study astrology to become qualified. Furthermore, an astrologer must be engaged on the spiritual path of self-realization, for this is the real goal of life. An astrologer who does have this clarity of perception can help a person by guiding them in what actions to perform to be successful in various areas of life and the best times to effect them.

Having your horoscope done should help you to make the right choices in life to gain success in all you desire. Action shapes destiny and our actions will determine the actual manifestation of karma, good and bad. The more knowledge gained, the more self-direction of destiny for true fulfilment in life, materially and spiritually. It is said in the vedic scriptures, which contain all sciences of life, including the astrological science, that knowledge is likened to a torchlight and fear and ignorance to darkness. The torchlight of knowledge illuminates the darkness of ignorance, thereby dissipating fear. When a person is in knowledge there is no fear, even at the point of death, or leaving the body. For those in true knowledge death is no more than another step on the path of life. Therefore human beings must gain knowledge in order to have happiness and peace of mind, in any and all circumstances.

I have divided this book into three parts. Part one is concerned with the practical applications of this science in different areas of life. Part two gives descriptions of the characteristics and representations of the planets, signs, houses and stars. This can be used to understand your own chart as well as in gaining basic knowledge of their meanings. Part three is concerned with remedial measures to help balance disharmonic influences within the horoscope.

It is my sincere hope that this book may be of value in helping to throw some light on the practical uses for having an astrological horoscope done and for further understandings of its meaning. Hopefully, one day this great science will again be given the respect it justly deserves and be utilized to the benefit of all humanity, as it formerly was and still is, in much of the Eastern world.

Sun

PART ONE

VEDIC ASTROLOGY:

YOUR PERSONAL ROADMAP TO SUCCESS

Moon

PHYSICAL HEALTH

Everyone is concerned with their health as well they should be. If you do not maintain your body properly then disease naturally has an open door to enter. Many of us put the emphasis on our physical health nowadays but, unless you have good mental & emotional health, you will still not feel whole or healthy. Even if you take care of your body and also study to develop a healthy mind, you will still feel incomplete without developing spiritual health. In the eternal scheme of things we are spirit, not matter - with which we seem to constantly identify. How to be healthy spiritually is a matter of grave importance.

First let us look at how astrology can help us understand inherent weaknesses in ourselves physically and mentally. Different "planets" rule over different parts of the body. Different "signs" have influence on particular areas of the body and the different "houses" also indicate the same. Therefore, by proper consideration of a birth chart horoscope, it is possible to ascertain physical and mental problems that you are likely to incur at various times of life. We can also see chronic difficulties that may arise during a lifetime, physically and psychologically.

Having knowledge of what difficulties we may have with our bodies and minds allows us to take preventive measures to allay the problems, or to greatly reduce their effects.

Vedic astrology provides a key to the diagnosis and prevention of disease far beyond the scope of modern medical science. Were modern doctors to also take advantage of medical astrology they could forsee what diseases a person is likely to contract in his or her lifetime, what parts of the body are likely to be affected and when they might be likely to occur. This most important branch of astrology has been used for thousands of years with astounding accuracy. Still today, in modern India, many ayur-vedic doctors use the combination of stethoscope and horoscope to make their diagnosis of patients ailments.

Modern medical science has successfully found cures for many diseases and developed vaccines to prevent epidemic diseases. Astrology can go a giant step further by allowing a qualified practitioner to diagnose weaknesses of the physical body and to predict specific ailments that may be contracted simply by careful study of the birth chart. With this knowledge a parent can institute preventive measures to protect a child from contracting certain illnesses right from infancy, rather than waiting until the malady becomes evident and thus requires curative measures. Doesn't it make more sense to prevent disease, if there is the knowledge of what diseases may occur, than to just rely on medicine for a cure once the disease rears it's ugly head? If an astrologer is also trained in anatomy, physiology and pathology he can use the horoscope to greater advantage than the stethoscope. The stethoscope is also a valuable tool, but the horoscope is much more valuable for understanding a person's future health,.

The strength of a horoscope in general will indicate the strength of the body and its ability to resist disease. There are certain "yogas", or combinations of planets, which serve to give excellent health. By the same token there are "yogas", or combinations, which can cause chronic suffering from different types of diseases. Planets each have different parts of the body that they "rule", or have jurisdiction, over. This means they will also affect specific bodily functions. The "signs" of the zodiac also affect specific areas of the body, individually.

The "houses" of a chart not only rule over different areas of life, but different parts of the body and their susceptibility to disease. In addition, the "signs" or constellations of stars (nakshatras) are extremely important in understanding specific affectations of disease and the times of occurrence.

An astrologer must study the birth chart of an individual, then the daily movements of the planets, to understand and diagnose present and future health.

The "Ayurveda", India's ancient medical texts, translated as the "science of life", are inextricably intertwined with the "Jyotish", the vedic astrological texts. In olden times, all ayurvedic doctors in India were also astrologers. The combination of these two sciences allowed them a complete system for diagnosis and treatment of not only diseases of the body but also of the mind. Note that even the twelve basic salts of homeopathy are associated and related to the twelve houses of the zodiac.

It follows that mental health can also be understood from a person's horoscope. There are many factors and planetary conjunctions that can indicate a troubled mind, neurosis, or psychosis. The psychological condition as a whole can be understood through a careful study of the birth chart. Even appearance and longevity of life can be accurately foretold. Therefore an astrologer must not only understand which planets cause disease but also the types that may manifest themselves, what areas of the body they will affect and when. Furthermore, he must also be well versed in the medical sciences and the natures of different diseases, as well as their symptoms.

Why is it that a robust-looking person will be said to be healthy by a doctor, yet come down with a debilitating illness not able to be foreseen by modern doctors? Why can a frailer, less-healthy appearing person combat and resist certain diseases? The answer is fate....karma. Everything about the future can be indicated by an individual's horoscope.

Does this mean that all is predestined and we cannot do anything to thwart future problems with the mind and body? No, it does not. Medical astrology can give great insights as to a proper diet for an individual to follow to maintain optimum health.

Let's take a look at the universally applicable ways in which we can first keep a healthy body and mind. First of all different people need to eat different types of food according to their body type. Not everyone has the same type of body, or physical constitution, so different people require different foods in different quantities to be healthy. The environment in which they live and the type of work they do will also influence the dietary needs. The ayur-vedic system of medicine describes the types, symptoms, appearance, etc. and prescribes different types of foods. It also provides insights on herbs to take to prevent and combat disease. Then a horoscope will indicate the right type of place for an individual to live for optimum health, as well as an occupation that is congruent with his/her mental and physical constitution. There are also spiritual practices that should be undertaken to balance physical, mental and spiritual health. Remedial measures, such as gemstones, may also be used to balance and harmonize planetary influences. (See Part 3). Without going into the actual science of ayur-veda to a great degree I cannot do it justice but I will discuss the universal truths in this regard.

In today's world much of the populace creates disease by lack of knowledge on eating. Fast food restaurants started in the U.S.A. and have spread throughout the world. Some medical and scientific research suggests that such processed foods may be responsible for much of the cancers and heart disease which are now world-wide, although the U.S.A. is still the leader. It is necessary to eat wholesome fresh fruits, vegetables, grains, beans, nuts, etc. to properly maintain the body. Meats are unsuitable for most people and in general flesh foods should never be eaten by anyone. Except in rare cases, flesh foods are prohibited for human society, as delineated in India's ancient vedic scriptures. The original precepts of most of the world's ancient religions and cultures espoused this identical principle. Even the old testament of Judaism gives this most important instruction of what foods should be used for human consumption.

Ignorance of this is at the root of today's health problems. Animal protein is easily available from milk products which can be obtained without slaughtering cows. So many wonderful foods can be prepared from the produce of the earth that fully maintain a healthy body.

There are so many people today that have realized the health benefits of being a vegetarian. There are wonderful books about diet that no doubt you've already read, or at least heard about. Even medical doctors are propounding giving up meat-eating to reduce cancer and heart disease. We've seen amazing changes in patients with incurable or undiagnosable illnesses for the better when simply switching to a vegetarian diet. I doubt there are many alive today that would refute the health benefits of vegetarianism. We are more concerned about our physical health today as we see the futility in lifestyles that destroy our bodies. More than ever you will see that people are exercising their bodies and minds to maintain physical and mental health. The fact is when we're really healthy in mind and body we feel happy. Isn't that what it's all about, feeling happiness? There is no amount of money or material success that will buy it. Vegetarians feel better, live longer and lead less stressful lives. This amounts to more peace of mind and body.

However, there is a further meaning of vegetarianism. We understand from the sages of ancient vedic times in India that vegetarianism was a prerequisite for being eligible to learn from a bona-fide guru of the eternal spiritual side of life. There is actually a verse in the "puranas" that says there is a specific part of the brain that can only be used if one is a vegetarian. They said that this part of the brain allowed them to perform physical austerities for advancement in the yoga system without the danger of prematurely leaving the body or, put plainly, so they wouldn't die from not eating or keeping their bodies in one position with a slowed heart rate for so long. These yogis would develop mystic siddhis, or powers, as a byproduct of their spiritual practice. It was not the goal of their austerities and spiritual practice.

So there must be a very real and important reason, spiritually, for not eating meat. That reason is nonviolence. The commandment "Thou shalt not kill" does not mean only people. We have no right to take the lives of poor innocent creatures for the satisfaction of our palate. There is nobody in this part of the world who could make an argument that there are not enough other foodstuffs. We have an abundance of fruits, vegetables, grains, nuts, beans, spices, even the milk of cows and goats. We are talking spiritually, now. It is not necessary to kill them for milk. In India the cow is considered one of the sacred mothers of the human race. The reason is because of nurturing us with her milk. In India dozens of products and dishes are made with milk products that delight even the most discriminating palate. So why should we kill poor animals for food unnecessarily? It is a crime and degrades the whole of human society.

When we realize that we are actually spirit soul, inhabiting this body for a short time, we thus realize that all living entities are spirit soul, inhabiting different bodies. It is said that there are 8,400,00 species of life in the material world. There are many variations within the lower of the species, as well. Most of us have taken countless births before this one. You only identify yourself as John, Robert, Mary, George, Rajiv, Mustaffa or whatever, due to your identifying with this incarnation. Actually you are not the person you call yourself. You are not your body. When the body ends, you will still exist. In the Bhagavad-Gita it says: "Never was there a time when you and I did not exist, nor all these kings". We are eternal, sentient beings. These bodies are only temporary manifestations. When the body is old and can no longer be used, you will cast it off like an old shirt, leaving it ,ultimately, to take a new one. So, in reality, animals are also our brothers. It is our duty to protect those that need protection, not slaughter them. When all life is respected, then it is possible to find out the real meaning of life. Vegetarianism is the most important of the true tenets of all forms of spirituality.

As long as the illusion that love is meant only for human beings exists, then there will be no realization of love at all and universal love is the most important lesson to be learned in life. If you learn how to feel love, to give love, to receive love, you will become happier than you knew was possible.

We human beings are meant to rule the earth but with love, not violence. Violence has it's place only because there is a lack of spiritual realization among the masses. With a spiritual awakening we can change the world to bring peace and love, where before there existed war and hatred.

God has many names, forms and attributes. God is worshiped in different ways, in different places, by different peoples. We can see the differences and we can see the similarities. The constant similarity is the teaching of love. How can you love if you are engaged in violence? Think about it! This was the hidden secret of all advanced ancient civilizations that endured for any length of time. It shall, in future centuries be known as the hidden secret that saved all human society from destruction.

Environment is another factor that causes health problems due to toxins in the air we breathe, the water we drink and even the agricultural products that we eat. It is possible to purify your water with the aid of a good water purifier and organically grown produce is available, to some degree. If the air is extremely bad where you live, then you may want to consider an air purifier, which can at least be effective when you are indoors.

The other factors to developing a healthy body are rest and exercise. It is important to regulate your sleeping habits. You must get enough sleep for your body and mind to function properly, six to eight hours a night are usually sufficient for most. Children need more sleep when growing, yet some adults can function well with as little as four to five hours nightly. The principle is that you must get enough rest depending on age and activity. Oversleeping is actually detrimental and serves to makes us feel tired, rather than refreshed.

Exercise is the other factor. Today much of the world lives in urban areas and does work that is not sufficient to physically exercise the body adequately. It doesn't matter whether you do hatha yoga, calisthenics, running or walking, Tai-Chi, martial arts, etc., but you must do something. Living the sedentary lifestyle that many live in western cities creates physical stagnation in the muscles, joints, respiratory system and internal organs. Even the brain functions better. Exercise also has the effect of making you feel good, or enlivened, mentally. Anyone who exercises would undoubtably agree with this point.

It follows that proper diet, rest and exercise are necessary to keep your physical health. Natural additives (vitamins, etc.) may be added to compensate for the lack of complete nutrition in our food. It goes without saying (but I'll say it anyway) that drugs and alcohol consumption greatly serve to deteriorate physical and psychological health, as well as shorten the lifespan. We generally give an indication of the lifespan when doing a horoscope but, according to lifestyle, this may be reduced considerably. Therefore, through a combination of the horoscope (to give us the information of inherent physical weaknesses of the body) and a knowledge of how to maintain the body properly (through proper diet, rest and exercise), everyone can enjoy good health to the limit of their circumstance.

Mental, emotional and psychological health must also be maintained through proper action. The only way to act properly is with knowledge. Good mental and emotional health is inextricably intertwined with spiritual health, for how can a person be emotionally well-balanced without understanding their true spiritual nature?

Mars

MENTAL, EMOTIONAL AND SPIRITUAL HEALTH

In order to maintain a healthy mind we must realize the true realities of life. Therefore we must consider our spiritual nature to understand the subtleties of mind, intelligence and ego. Accordingly mental, emotional and spiritual health go together and, unless you have some knowledge in this regard, you cannot stop the onslaught of negative emotions brought on by ignorance and fear. We not only need to engage ourselves in some sort of fulfiling work to occupy our minds but need to understand why we fall victim to feelings of hate, envy, greed and avarice. These emotions only serve to destroy us intellectually, psychologically, emotionally and spiritually. Why is there so much hate in the world, anyway?

In Germany and even in other countries, the resurgence of racism is alarming. Young men roam the streets, organized and unorganized, burning, looting, robbing, raping, pillaging. In Germany the cry from these men is to oust all foreigners, Jews and anyone else they decide to vent their fury upon. In Bosnia-Herzegovina it is Serb against Muslim and Croat, as well as Croat against Muslim. In the Middle-East it is Jew against Muslim, as well as Muslim against Christian. In China's territories the hate is directed against Tibet, or any that will not "kowtow". In India it is Muslim versus Hindu. In Europe and the United States it's white hating black and, depending on time and circumstance, many different groups finding reason to hate each other.

Are we heading toward a time in the near future when we will destroy ourselves? It is seen that the greed of man is truly causing destruction to our very planet! The blood of the earth, oil, is being constantly pumped out to fuel man's passion for an energy source that not only is finite but, in the process, the byproducts are polluting our oceans, rivers, skies and the very air we breathe. These and the byproducts of other chemical production are polluting the world we live in, irreparably......at least that world that which we and many generations to come shall know. Besides hate, greed is the most blinding of emotions.

What events will transpire, resulting from the proliferation of nuclear weapons around the world, to further destroy our planet? Do not be so naive as to think that they are not now in the hands of those that would use them without consideration of the results. It has been predicted by astrologers for many, many years that there will be great, horrific happenings for the world before the turn of this century. The predictions range from nuclear war to earthquakes, tidal waves to volcanoes erupting around the globe. One thing is sure, whether the descriptions purported by Nostradamous, Sage Brghu or the many modern psychics and astrologers, there will be some difficult karma for the planet before the 1990's are over. Is it all predestined? Is there nothing that can be done about it?

Hate exists due to illusion. Men become frustrated in their attempts to rule nature and to enjoy the gratification of their physical senses. The illusion that"I am the master of all I survey" permeates all societies today on the planet. As any happiness is always temporary and must be interspersed with varying amounts of distress, they turn on each other in frustration. They blame the other's very existence for causing their material maladies. Then there is escalation of this illusion, fed by the false ego which tells them they are better than anyone else. Men are actually so arrogant as to believe that, by dint of their country of origin, race, or creed, they are superior to another. This is pure illusion.

The reality is that we are not English, French, Russian, Jew, Muslim, African, etc. These are bodily designations having nothing to do with who we really are. As an astrologer I examine a person's horoscope to see what karma they have brought with them to this birth in the present body. What pleasures will be enjoyed and what pains must be endured are told there. The very number of breaths we are allotted during this life, thus determining our life span, is also told. You may today be English and, having grown up in "merrie old England", are quite attached to home and country. When returning after being away for some time, you feel a feeling of gladness to be back "home" and thus some sense of satisfaction. This very feeling is felt by all other peoples around the world, whether in India, Sweden, Brazil, or Switzerland. Everyone identifies, to some degree, with their place of birth being somehow superior or special. Everyone is in this same illusion.

A human being is, in fact, capable of degrading himself so far that he is not even offered a chance at another human birth for the next "body". It can be that a person who lives "like a pig" in this life, misusing the great boon of human life which is meant to acquire knowledge, takes the body of a pig in the next life. Whatever the body, it is not really US. We are not the bodies we presently dwell in, nor any we have inhabited in past lives, nor any we may be born into in future lives. We are spiritual sparks, known as the soul, which is never born nor dies and can never be extinguished. WE are eternal - these bodies are not. They are given to allow us to fulfil our desires for sense gratification exclusively, or to allow us to act in ways that will enable us to gain knowledge of our true identities and duties as human beings. The culmination is to find out the solution for the real problems of birth, death, old age and disease. Nobody wants to become ill, grow old, or die but it is assured that we must.

So is there a force to combat this great power of illusion that causes men to hate each other to the point of wanting to enslave or annihilate? Is there a way to soften the blow of this karma that is predestined to cause malefic happenings to befall us? There is - LOVE is the answer. Only love can destroy hatred. Only knowledge can destroy ignorance and illusion. If the leaders of our societies will not listen and heed this call to sanity before it is too late, then we must do all we can on our own. Awareness of our true spiritual identity will dispel the illusions we live in due to identification solely with our bodies. Why must men always wish to control with unlimited power? It is unfulfilable lust and greed to possess more than is necessary, to control others and what they may temporarily possess that causes hatred.

Without a spiritual renaissance we are hurtling to our destruction. Even in this men are so arrogant as to believe that the religion of THEIR country is the only true one, that only the name THEY utter is the true way of addressing the supreme. You and I have but one, or, at most, a few names we are called by. But is this true also of God, the Supreme?! If God is omnipotent than God is also unlimited. God takes so many forms and is worshiped in so many ways throughout the world. Therefore being omnipotent and unlimited, the source of all that is, God can have unlimited names, unlimited potencies, unlimited forms. God is seen by some as Allah, Jehovah, Krishna, Rama, or Buddha. God is seen by some in the majesty of nature's beauty in rivers, mountains, rainbows, or in the "fury of providence" in earthquakes or other natural disturbances, even described in insurance company clauses as "acts of God". Hate, war, destruction of our environment and the lives of our fellow man due to ignorance are not "acts of God". These are the results of the desires of those most firmly enmeshed in the illusion that they are their bodies, the desire to enjoy sense gratification and a false sense of superiority, based on their particular bodily designation.

What of the mental depression that seems to plague so many people, almost, if not completely, robbing them of good quality of life? Did you know that in the West as much as 68% of women, and 42% of men, find themselves dealing with mental depression at some point in their lives? What causes depression and how can it be dealt with? Most people are able to continue with their duties in life and learn to bear this feeling without having it completely take them over, yet a percentage find it absolutely necessary to seek some form of help, from counselling to actually being institutionalized. Why do we get depressed for seemingly nothing special sometimes? Of course we all have to deal with sadness and disappointments in life, but often depression occurs without any particular circumstance being the sole catalyst, just a general feeling of unhappiness and unfulfilment, leading, in extreme cases, to utter hopelessness and, sometimes, suicide. In today's modern world depression is becoming more and more of a problem for many people, especially in the Western world, where so-called scientifically advanced civilization is centred. What is so wrong with the way we live that mental health seems to be deteriorating in so many of us?

The United States and Western Europe have the most burgeoning mental health businesses in the world. Virtually tens of thousands of people, seemingly successful in their lives, are regularly visiting psychologists, psychiatrists, psychoanalysts and similar practitioners. Furthermore this is in countries that have the highest standards of living in the world. As a matter of fact those that have the highest instances of depression have no lacking in the necessities of life. However, if you go to countries in Asia, even to economically deprived places within India etc. you find that people are not so troubled mentally and clinical depression, neurosis and psychosis are relatively rare. Why in the places where the greatest strides have been made scientifically are there the greatest amount of mental health problems?

The reason is the difference in philosophical outlooks on life in the world. In the West we are an almost fatalistic society, putting all our concentration on success in this life materially. Death and what occurs during and after this transition is rarely spoken of. Most people don't want to think about it, let alone make some effort to learn how to prepare while they are alive in these bodies. Nevertheless, no matter how much money and possessions you accumulate, how many friends and lovers you have, or how close knit your family, city, or country, there is always a nagging feeling of "is this all there is to life?". I know so many people around the world that, although extremely prosperous materially, are also extremely unsatisfied. Most of us have our ideas of what it would take to make us happy in life and generally it centres on financial independence or wealth-building and relationships, yet, once achieved, there's an almost immediate letdown. We thought we would experience some form of bliss from the attainment of material goals and then find out it is short-lived. So what is the missing link, the key to being able to gain happiness in life?

It lies in understanding our true nature as spirit and making spiritual, as well as material advancement, while we are here. We cannot neglect either or we cannot attain any lasting satisfaction. There must be a balance of physical, mental and spiritual health. We must ask ourselves questions like "who am I, really?" "who is God?" "what is the goal of human life?" "where have I come from and where am I going after this life"?

With spiritual recognition there comes hopefulness, rather than hopelessness. We are born into these bodies carrying our karma from previous incarnations with us. When we die, or leave this body, that is all we will take with us. All of our possessions and relationships, based on bodily identification, will be finished at the time of death. Therefore it is useless to make plans to stay here forever. Although Westerners don't like to discuss this, no one can deny that he or she will grow old and die. We must find out how to gain knowledge of the soul and what is our true desire above and beyond our bodily identifications. Fear is born of ignorance and it is said that knowledge is the torchlight which dispels the darkness of ignorance. Because in India and many other Eastern countries there is at least some understanding of karma and reincarnation, or transmigration of the soul, there is much less mental sickness among the populace. People understand that this life is not the end and that only self-realization can bring happiness and peace of mind. We must give greater concentration to that which is our eternal position in life, not just concentrating on things based on our bodies, which are temporary.

More important than this is "action" in the present life. Action shapes destiny. Our work in this lifetime not only creates karma for future lifetimes but shapes the present destiny shown by the astrological horoscope. Action, or activities, is therefore the deciding factor, in determining how this lifetime will actually turn out. Proper action can greatly lessen the effects of "negative" karma, resulting from activities performed in ignorance in a previous life and it can also increase "positive" karma, earned through activities performed in knowledge, or goodness, in a previous incarnation.

Accordingly astrology is meant to make us think about our true spiritual nature and what our "real" activities should be, for the true goal of human life is spiritual knowledge, leading to transcendence of the material stratosphere. What is the point of repeating birth after birth, only to become immersed in materialism time and time again? If I must give up everything I've worked so hard for in this life at the time of death, then my work in acquiring material things is obviously not the goal. Any sane person can understand that at the time of death, everything in relation to the present body is finished. We cannot take anything of this world with us. Therefore, it should lead us on a quest to discover transcendence, or our spiritual nature, for this is eternal. What activities will lead to discovering the truth of life and of true self? In other words what activities will guide you on the path of self-realization? If material activities only produce that which is impermanent and we are actually eternal living beings, there must be activities that will produce results of a permanent nature. Results that can go to the next life at the time of death.

The real message and usefulness of the holy science of astrology is to cause an awareness of and interest in spiritual contemplation. It is of the utmost importance in life that we begin to discover our true selves and our true nature of happiness and love. How to do so? The Vedas give so many ways of advancing on the path, as do the higher precepts of all religions.

Begin by asking the most important questions of life. The real problems of material life are birth, death, old age and disease. Is there a way to solve these problems? Most assuredly there is and it is our birthright to know these answers. Think about it, seek out a lecture or attend a seminar on Vedic astrology. This will put you on a path from which you'll never want to stray. The path to perfect physical, mental and spiritual health. We must learn to balance all three to live a complete, happy and satisfying life.

The science of vedic astrology is a great tool for helping us to understand ourselves as spiritual entities who have taken these bodies due to our own previous actions. Whatever one does, good or bad, creates karma. Good actions will allow one to take a desirable body and be granted material pleasures. This can mean rebirth in a "well-to-do" or religious family, on this planet or in promotion to planets beyond this universe where the conditions are far more "heavenly" than we experience here on earth. Harmful actions will ensure a more miserable birth in the next life. From horoscopes we can tell so much about ourselves and therefore make proper decisions in life to make advancement, not only to ensure material happiness but to gain some degree of spiritual happiness, building and advancing in spiritual consciousness from birth to birth. Only then can we successfully deal with depression and its debilitating effects on human life.

To gain spiritual happiness, or spiritual knowledge, requires a bona-fide teacher, or "guru", as they are often termed, that is sufficiently advanced to be able to impart spiritual knowledge to others. Such teachers are not easily found so, whatever your beliefs or particular inclinations in philosophy and religion, give these more importance in your life. Seek answers from a higher source. In countries where simple living and high thinking are prevalent there is a more pervasive atmosphere of satisfaction in life. Think about it, then do something about it. We are "piloting our own planes" in this lifetime. If you seek truth, you will find it. Your action shapes your destiny, so it's up to you. By adopting such an attitude of mind and by associating with more spiritually inclined companions you will have a greater chance of finding answers and meeting those from whom you can learn. Question everything to be sure you are not being "milked" by the unscrupulous. The best test is that no true teacher is out to make a substantial material gain from students, for to do so would only create bad karma for the teacher.

So what will be the outcome? Will love win out over hate and make the earth a paradise, as some believe? Unfortunately, the answer is no. It is not possible to change those that are hell bent on their own destruction, as well as the destruction of our planet, to achieve their selfish aims. But those of us that do have the spark of love within our hearts can fan that spark into a flame and, eventually, into a raging inferno. We can combat the hatred in the world by spreading as much love to all we can. It is the most powerful force, capable of changing the face of the world. We cannot get rid of the hatred that permeates those in ignorance completely but we can greatly reduce its influence by spreading love and good-will toward all we are able. In this way we have the chance of changing enough of the world and the consciousness of people to make a difference. How to start? Try to smile. Wish good on those around you, as well as yourself. Feel good about what you do and say, for we all know truth and right from wrong within our hearts. You will find yourself happy, healthy and well-adjusted in all spheres of life. Go in peace, or as they say in Hawaii.... "Aloha".

Mercury

RELATIONSHIP COMPATIBILITY USING ASTROLOGY

So many people nowadays are experiencing problems in their relationships and could well benefit by utilizing the science of astrology to understand themselves, as well as their partner, or prospective partner. When I'm asked to do compatibility charts for couples, I begin by doing each of their lifetime horoscopic charts. I will then compare the two using the eastern astrological system of comparison for marriage but most importantly I look at the two individuals, their goals in life and the way they think and act. These things can be understood by careful analysis of the horoscope.

Generally, when two people want to be together and are considering a more permanent relationship, there is already some love and affection. This is very important. There must be a genuine attraction, both sexual and otherwise, to be happy as a couple. Then there must be avenues for communication and understanding to achieve a lasting and fulfiling relationship. Being life partners is not all easy and simple, as we humans are emotional beings. The attitudes and thought patterns of the two people are what we need to be most concerned about. The initial infatuation eventually fades somewhat, so there must be realization that this will happen and you must share enough common ground to raise the relationship to higher and higher levels as life goes on.

Therefore each needs to understand the other's desires, mannerisms and ways of thinking in order to make a relationship work. I usually sit the two down for a private consultation, separately. The reason is to be able to give each a chance to look at themselves honestly and to let them try to understand their partner's mind, without comment from the partner during the consultation. I try to first get a person to look at themselves objectively, their goals and desires, what their true capabilities are and what they really are willing to sacrifice for the sake of a relationship. There is always some give and take to have a successful relationship, but our basic natures do not change. You must understand your own mind and the way you think. Then you can try to understand your partner's, for neither of you are going to change in that way. We are who we are. We have developed our personalities and natures over countless lifetimes, not just this one and you cannot do an "about-face" overnight. We can learn to change the way we speak at certain times, get control over our lower nature that may cause problems in our communication, or the way we externally react to the world, or learn new communication skills, but you cannot change your basic mental faculties, or your modes of perception. We can always improve ourselves but that must come from within.

If a person thinks they can "change" a prospective partner, they are mistaken. A person may allow themselves to be pushed or bullied but it only leads to resentment and dissatisfaction in the relationship. If you love someone, then try to understand and accept them as they are. Generally I point out how the other partner thinks in different areas and try to teach "personal" communication skills, meaning ways of communicating with each other to keep harmony in the relationship and definite "no-no's" not to use in communication.

We all have ways that we react, as individuals. The key to a successful relationship lies in communication. We may not be able to change our mental capacity and personality but everyone can learn good communication skills to improve the way they get along in all relationships, not just marital type ones. I try to point out the things that definitely will cause arguments and discord. These may be in ways of talking, acting, or reacting to things you might say or do. The things that will cause problems should be cerebral buttons, marked with a big, red X.... not to touch. The ways of speaking and acting that will promote greater harmony, should be practiced at every opportunity. Whilst we can learn to modify our behaviour, it's usually impossible to completely change basic nature.

One of the areas where I do a great deal of work is dealing with abusive relationships. If two people know the things that set each other off, they can learn how not to let it happen. Anger control is something that many people need to learn. Many times relationships start to break apart due to things people say to each other in anger. You don't have to say everything you think! If you have a problem with too much anger within your mind, learn to expel the negative energy in more constructive ways. If you are thinking, "you @#$&*%^&"......... DON'T say it!! Hold your tongue until you cool off. 99% of the time, in a short while, you will realize you didn't really mean the things you were thinking. It was just anger in your mind, often the root of which being something completely unrelated to your partner. If you did not blow up and say what you were thinking at that moment, then you'll have nothing to apologize for later. Your partner may forgive you for this type of intrusion, if it does happen, but they cannot forget. Think about it. How many times do couples fight about things they really don't care about,or hurt each other with words they later wish they had never said? Most couples ruin their relationship by saying things out of anger, or worse, by violent reactions leading to physical abuse.

In looking at a couple's compatibility I try to show each of them the buttons to push to make their partner feel good, loved and appreciated. Then I show them the buttons never to push if they want the relationship to last. By objectively learning more about what really makes the other tick, they can learn how to best react in certain situations and how not to react. Sometimes it's necessary to modify certain types of behaviour that a person has never even realized was not in their best interests, the best interests of others, or they were never aware of at all! After some practice, the new behavioural traits become second nature and don't require so much mental concentration. The result is that you become a better communicator, allowing you greater success in all endeavours of life involving other people. Remember that almost everything we do is 90% communication. After the consultation I then leave it up to the couple to decide if they can make this relationship work. Most of the time couples do, once they know how.

Generally I find that a couple that learns early on how to communicate efficiently and learn enough about what's inside each other's mind and heart, become determined to make their relationship work. It's not hard, because they are so much in love. Remember how easy it seemed in the beginning of your relationship to put up with almost anything? (Even your lover's less than becoming personal habits seemed cute! I'm sure everyone has had experience of this, at some time or another.)Therefore it's easier earlier on in a relationship to stave-off future problems, avoiding them as much as is humanly possible.

Obviously some matches are better than others. Two people that have similar ways of thinking will have less trouble getting along and understanding each other's motives in their actions. Those that are complete opposites and have completely different goals will find it much more difficult to make the relationship work, in the long run. The more information we have about our partner's likes, dislikes, goals in life, personality and basic way of thinking, the easier it is to modify somewhat certain ways of speaking or acting, to make communication more joyful between the two of you. Remember, you want to be able to talk to this person and be with this person for a lifetime. We all want to be loved, cared for and understood. We often have different ways of thinking or expressing ourselves and this is natural, because we are all individuals. Knowledge of how to most effectively communicate with the most important person in your life is vital to a successful relationship.

I have seen many couples derive new plateaus of understanding each other through the use of astrology. It enables them to gain deeper insights into each other's way of thinking, feeling, willing and acting, thus helping them to develop together in a way that is mutually satisfying and fulfiling. At the other extreme some compatibility charts help couples to realize that they could never modify their behaviour in such a way as to make it work. This shows the relationship in a proper light, possibly avoiding devastating consequences later.

Most couples learn things about each other and themselves that help them to communicate better and to not neglect the things that make the other's heart grow fonder. Love begins with physical attraction, most of the time, but making it blossom requires understanding, commitment and genuine compassion. Everyone can make their relationships work, if they have the skills and knowledge to do so. Everyone wants to be happy but it's up to us to do something about it. Learn the keys to a happy and fulfiling relationship. Do it for the sake of yourself and that special someone, who will certainly come into your life one day, if they have not already.

Jupiter

HUMAN SEXUALITY

A discussion of human sexuality inevitably leads to an analysis of what traits are inherently male and which are inherently female. Yin and yang, as the two energies are termed in Chinese philosophy, are present in us all. This is seen in our physical bodies and projected through our personalities to reflect the inner desires. In today's world the mixture of yin and yang in both males and females seems to be in many cases, almost equal, with a leaning toward the feminine side in most women and more so toward the male side, in the cases of most men.

The incidence of homosexuality also seems to be greater than ever before in history. Are women more yang and have men begun to experience feelings and emotions that are more yin than previously known? Are there more gays and lesbians born now? Why is it that, in general, homosexuals are actually born with an inherent "same sex" desire for sexual relationships and why do they seem to be overly endowed with traits of the opposite gender? To begin with we must examine how we come into these human forms and how it happens that we are born male or female.

As previously stated the astrological science is based on the spiritual science of transmigration of the soul, or reincarnation. We are spirit souls. Our gender is understood on the basis of what body we happen to be born into in this life. Most of us have had countless births previous to this one we are presently living and have been in the both gender bodies. In the case of many homosexuals it is seen that an opposite gender personality exists from that of the physical body. By charting an astrological horoscope based on a person's time of birth, date of birth and place of birth, we can understand the predetermined destiny of someone. How is this possible? It is because we choose our conditions of life due to our desires and how we try to fulfil them in life. It shows what the destiny of a person is and how easy or difficult it will be to alter it or to push it beyond perceived limits. Actions determine how destiny unfolds, so an astrological horoscope will show what actions should be taken up by the person to fulfil desires, materially and spiritually. According to the individual's karma different actions will be easier or more difficult to perform and results will be easier or more difficult to attain. Action is the key factor here, once you have an in depth perspective based on the horoscope, but certain things may be beyond the reach or scope of a person.

It seems that throughout history men had certain clearly defined roles in society, as did women. There was not such a close equality in many circumstances as we see today. Why is that? The reason is due to the changing world and the definition of gender responsibility changing. Men and women have had to change to survive. As these changes occur from birth to birth, especially psychologically, women learn to develop male traits to be able to fulfil their own desires. Men do as well, in the other direction. We learn from the "Vedas" that men would care for women, see to it that they were protected and that their desires were fulfiled, to as great a degree as possible. Women were respected and revered. They were protected as children by their fathers and family, by their husbands in marriage and by their sons when in old age. Women were able to live happily and peacefully. They could trust and believe in their men and a spiritual basis for life was ever realized. There was peace and harmony between the sexes. Men fulfiled their responsibilities toward women, themselves, their families, communities and, above all else, the responsibility to act in accordance with the laws of nature. Women would care for and nurture their men and fulfil their own responsibilities to themselves, their children and the community. They were not forced to take an independent stand. They were not used or abused, therefore they did not have the same fears and anxieties currently prevalent. Children were not solely their responsibility either, as it often turns out today, as an unfortunate result of divorce.

In the modern world things are vastly different and these very clearly defined lines between the sexes have all but disappeared. Men have taken an attitude of less and less responsibility toward women, their progeny, community, etc. If women didn't learn to fend for themselves they would be completely lost. Women have also taken an attitude, especially here in the West, of wanting to deal in the so called "world of men" in work, business and the market-place. To be able to accomplish this they must develop their inherent maleness to a greater degree. There are no longer any clear cut lines. Often it's sink or swim. Nobody else is there to do it for you.

So how do we deal with these differences in expression of sexuality to make our personal, intimate relationships succeed? Astrology can provide great insights to allow a person to understand themselves and their needs more objectively, thus developing more of a balance to be able to succeed in relationships. Partners can objectively understand each other, learn to respect the strengths and not exploit the weaknesses in each other. There is such an almost equal mixture of yin and yang today in many people, especially externally in the roles of women, that to understand yourself objectively through astrology can go a long way in boosting self esteem and comfort with your own being. If you are well adjusted and happier with yourself, not feeling that you should be different, then you can be more open and supportive of a partner, gaining greater fulfilment in a relationship.

I do many horoscopes for women where there is a very strong Mars in the birth chart, indicating great strength to accomplish things in this world and little likelihood that these women will want to surrender to a man's ideas of what they should be like, or how they should relate to others in the world. Why should they, anyway? In my work I find more women searching and contemplating how to help themselves and the world in general than ever before. Slowly, but surely, I see more men opening up to change and dealing with their feminine emotional side, also to make positive changes needed in their lives. The reasons are more difficult to pinpoint but it is obvious that we humans need tools to help us understand ourselves, our desires and our positions in this world. The more you know about yourself, where you've come from and where your present course is taking you, the more able you will be to act in such a way as to direct your own destiny. Problems of sexuality can be understood and dealt with, changing them from detriments to assets We can learn how best to direct ourselves, using all the inherent qualities with which we are born. The problems are born of ignorance; the solutions are born of knowledge. Gain knowledge of yourself and you will assuredly be able to get all out of life that you possibly can.

DISCOVERING YOUR POTENTIAL & CHOOSING A CAREER

Today there seems to be a plethora of self-help programmes for unleashing inner potentials, developing self-confidence and learning to not be your own hindrance in life. There are even some that tout their own particular "get rich" scheme, showing themselves to be an example of why "anyone can do it". These programmes are not cheap. There is an array of hands-on seminars, lectures, tapes, books, etc. that are said, by their creators, to give anyone the training to become successful, either in a particular field, or just in general. In essence, many of these self-help programmes teach worthy concepts of positive thinking and self-determination.

I have met many people that have sent away for these programmes after seeing a very powerful television marketing tool known as an "infomercial". These are very popular today, especially in America. Depending on a person's skills and fund of knowledge in general, the actual product is reviewed by customers from "something I already knew" to "it changed my life". The general self-help programmes have some value but, in the case of those that teach a specific method of earning or a particular business (such as property investment), they will not work in all cases. These programmes are based on the premise that anyone can achieve success at this same engagement, if only someone shows you how. In fact, this is not possible.

An individual's horoscope reveals what the potential is for career success as well as for wealth-building. What types of engagements would be successful is also seen. One thing to remember is that we are all individuals. We maintain this individuality always, in life and in death. Your existence is always seen to have individuality. Some of us are, more or less, emotional beings, have different degrees of logic and, of course, have distinct likes and dislikes according to our perceptions of life. Through the use of astrology we can understand not only a person's nature, but concentrate on what actions would bring about the greatest degrees of success. Due to being individuals with different ways of thinking, feeling and willing, we don't all do things the same way. It would be an awfully boring world if we were all the same. "Different strokes for different folks" is an adage that generally rings true.

Whether it is in career, marriage or whatever, having your horoscope to use as a guide is an invaluable tool. When you have knowledge of what to do, how to go about it and at what time, your chances of success are greatly increased. Through the birth chart we can make an analysis of exactly which courses of action will be along the path of least resistance. Then we can learn the skills, use self-help programmes to improve our confidence and communication skills, if necessary, thereby operating at our peak "personal power". Often you had a good deal of this knowledge within you but it took the validation through the horoscope to allow you to accept it. You are then more able to capitalize on your strengths in learning further skills to achieve your ambitions in all spheres of life, physical, emotional and spiritual.

Many positions within a horoscope suggest success in fields from medicine to law, to real property, to all sorts of things. What one person can succeed in is not necessarily the same thing in which another can achieve success. If you engage in something that you enjoy and feel comfortable doing, you will, naturally, be more successful. Let's reflect on just how most of us go about taking a career direction and making this important decision that will affect how we spend most of our waking hours for the rest of this life.

Until the twentieth century boys would generally go into whatever field or business their fathers were in, or were apprentices to someone the family knew, in order to learn a trade. It was more or less determined by birth what career you would undertake to earn a livelihood. Girls were, for the most part, brought up learning to cook, sew, take care of a house and children, etc. It was accepted that they would marry and dedicate their lives to their family. It was rare that a woman chose to do another engagement and society frowned upon it, which would make it all the more difficult to do.

Today the world is a different place. Young men and women don't usually know what they want to do until they are older, sometimes not until they've reached their late twenties and even then many haven't made a decision as to a career. Our society allows greater freedom of choice in everything, for both the sexes. Many young people finish higher education with a degree and find that they still aren't sure what they want to do, or that they cannot get employment in their chosen field. How is someone to make an intelligent choice as to a career direction? Often young people aren't particularly attracted to any particular job or field and they just eventually randomly pick something. They need money for the necessities of life, just like their parents and grandparents before them. Therefore, often by their forties, many feel unfulfilled in their careers and are frustrated by being forced to continue doing something they have no desire to do. I say forced because, by then, most adults have financial responsibilities to family, etc. and it's not possible to start again, even if they did know what they'd be happier doing.

Astrology can show us directions to take in our career that will be easier, more profitable and generally more fulfiling. Wouldn't it be nice to know this when deciding on a career? When people do something that is in keeping with their nature and they find it interesting, or challenging, they gain greater peace of mind. What could be more wonderful than that and what a blessing to be able to avert choices that may ultimately lead to boredom, dissatisfaction, or failure? Doing something that you have the most potential of succeeding in gives the greatest chance of satisfaction and fulfilment. How many people do you know that work at jobs that they hate or, at best, simply tolerate out of necessity? Wouldn't it be nice to be able to do something that you find not only interesting but that you actually enjoy? Think about how much time in our lives is spent at our employment. Instead of feeling unfulfilled, or cheated by destiny, why not find out what types of work would be not only more interesting but would bring you the most success? Usually today we choose an occupation on the basis of pay, but not everyone that does the same thing gets the same pay, nor feels as satisfied doing their job. Successfully choosing a fulfiling career that offers one the greatest chance of success is another example of how astrology can make a practical difference in our lives, those of our children, other loved ones or friends.

PROSPERITY AND POSITIVE THINKING DOES IT REALLY WORK?

Today there are so many programmes for success and prosperity through positive thinking and mental determination. There are many practitioners who use a myriad of terms to describe their form of manifesting your desires through the power of your mind. Does it really work? If so, how does it work? Can you get anything you want by being determined mentally?

As I've stated many times before, not everyone can be successful at the same thing, nor attain their success following the exact same programme. We are, eternally, individuals as spirit souls and here, on earth, in our bodily forms. Conjunctions in certain persons' charts make success likely in certain areas of business or employment, whereas others would have an extremely hard time. Therefore I try to steer a person in the direction of least resistance, as you might say.

What of the theory that positive thinking can make you successful and that to succeed you only require dedication and perseverance? The answer is that it does work. If you do not have the capacity to succeed easily in a certain area, your subconscious often knows this, regardless of the conscious mind. If you apply yourself religiously, in a disciplined fashion, using your mental faculties to visualize your success, you will most definitely attain success far beyond what would otherwise be possible. As you sow, so you shall reap. Therefore, if you're able to apply yourself 100%, your success is assured. This is not easy, though. It requires sincere dedication.

What do we mean by "prosperity"? If wealth building is what you're after, you will also have to gain the knowledge of business in general, product knowledge of what you're attempting to sell and of how to discipline yourself to attain your goals. Nothing comes without dedication; this is a key factor. One of the most important things is to dedicate yourself to something that you believe in. It's practically impossible to succeed at something, or truly believe in yourself and what you are doing if you don't like the activity. Next it requires total dedication, so be ready to give up almost everything else. Read books by famous businessmen and see how much time and effort they put into work. A man like Donald Trump sleeps only four hours a night and is engaged in some form of intense negotiations, planning, keeping up to date, etc. practically every waking hour. If this is what you want, try to follow the example of someone like this and see if it's possible. Though many people propound to desire great wealth, there are few that can put out the amount of energy to obtain it. Write down your goals and desires. Make a list of short-range goals, for this week, month and year. Then make a list of long range goals. Where do you want to be in one year, two years, five years, twenty years? Take a look at what you've written and see how practical the goals are. Then set yourself a daily discipline to get there. Success comes one day at a time, not overnight. Of course there are the exceptions where someone wins the "pools" or "premium bonds", but this is karma earned in a previous lifetime and, as such, is not a practical goal. You cannot work for it, or set it as a goal. If you did, your chances of success would be almost nil. However everyone can become successful and prosperous, through positive thinking. I have done horoscopes of people that were not very prosperous materially, but saw that they would attain this. Somehow by karma, they were afforded an opportunity and, when presented they had the wherewithal to take advantage of it. Then using the tools of positive thinking and visualization to spur them on, they became successful.

Wealth is not the only definition of "prosperity", or becoming "prosperous". Not everyone has the ability to become materially wealthy. As previously stated, material results are accorded due to actions not only in this life, but in previous lives. If you have performed the actions that will reap great future wealth, then it is possible. (Of course you must know what activities need to be performed to gain this boon in the future, whether in this life or the next.) Practically speaking it is doubtful that any one who is born into a meagre material situation and has not been afforded the necessary education and opportunities to get into business, can become wealthy. However, true success and prosperity means you are happy and satisfied. That is why ANYONE can attain success. Money is not the answer to happiness and wealth does not equate to fulfilment.

Prosperity is a feeling. It is a feeling of satisfaction with life. If you think positively in all that you do and push yourself toward your personal goals, you can easily attain this prosperity. The real key is within you, deep in your heart. There is one thing that if you possess it you will feel boundless in happiness, satisfaction and prosperity. This thing is LOVE. Love for yourself, your family, friends, community, country and all others in this world. Have you ever seen the look of satisfaction on parents' faces when engaged with their children in loving relations? This is love. Or the love between family members that are always there for each other? The love between two lovers or newlyweds? It is so strong because it is UNCONDITIONAL. There is not the expectation of anything in return, but LOVE. THIS IS THE MOST IMPORTANT THING ONE CAN LEARN IN THIS LIFE.

A so-called religionist, if not exhibiting love and compassion for fellow men and women, cannot begin to tap into "transcendental love". How do we achieve this topmost state of consciousness? Start by training yourself to wish everyone you meet good fortune and happiness. Not in words necessarily, but mentally. Wish peace and prosperity on all you meet. Rejoice in the good fortune of others, knowing that we are all part of one family in a spiritual sense. If you train your mind in this way, before very long it will come naturally. This will reduce your envy for the prosperity of others until you become a nonenvious person, filled with the joy of life. You will feel prosperous, happy and satisfied, regardless of how much material goods you have accumulated. Your mind will be positive in the mode of goodness and your wishing of good things to others will bring them to you.

Thinking positively and engaging yourself in your chosen profession will be satisfying. You will no longer spend all your waking moments hankering after more material success. You will have gained material success through your dedication, work, positive visualization and will feel happiness due to feeling love for others. Be the well-wisher of all and prosperity shall be yours. Utilize your talents, intelligence and mind to their utmost. Success and prosperity are your birthright. Claim them through right and positive thought and action. With the power of love you will attain "success" and true "prosperity" beyond your wildest dreams.

CONSCIOUSNESS AND SPIRITUALITY

There are three basic levels of consciousness that human beings exist in during their waking hours. The first and most fundamental level of consciousness is the sensual platform. This is a level where we are mostly concerned with pleasures enjoyed with our external senses. On this level we are thinking about the necessities of physical life and sense gratification. There is concern for eating and for sleeping, which is necessary, but often most people also consider it a great pleasure, especially to sleep for longer periods of time, when at all possible.

Then there is great emphasis put on sexuality. How we feel sexually and how we relate it to others. This is no doubt the most important thing in the world to most people, especially in youth. We worry about our appearance and how others view us. Much concentration is put on being a good lover and how sexually attractive we are. There is no doubt that, for many, this is the single most dominating thing that they worry about.

Then there is our defence mechanism. We work during life and accumulate possessions, families, friends, etc. We wish to protect these things so that we may enjoy them as long as possible. "As long as possible" is the key here as, whatever we accumulate on the sensual platform, however fit and strong the body may be, however attractive we are to others....... it is only temporary. The pleasures diminish from these things as our bodies age and our concern dwindles, as we experience discomfort and illnesses brought about by eternal time.

This sensual platform is a platform of consciousness that human beings share with the animal kingdom. Although people eat, sleep, mate and defend in a highly polished or, so-called "advanced", fashion, the animals also engage in these activities.

The next platform of consciousness is the intellectual platform. This is the platform on which we delve into the "why" and "wherefore" of this material world. We speculate and experiment with so many sciences pertaining to this world. We use our brains to develop ideas and solutions to problems, both of the body and the mind. In this mode we try to understand, with our minds, everything around us and sometimes within us. Intellectualism is necessary for man to create things and maintain them in this world for our use.

Philosophical thinking and religiosity also begin on the intellectual platform. Man uses his mind and whatever experience he has to ask questions and try to find answers. The intellect is used in every decision we make, constantly weighing possibilities and the "pros and cons" to everything. Science relies on intellectuals to test speculative theory to find answers. Empirical philosophers, who rely on their minds solely to understand philosophy and religion, are on this intellectual platform. They think about an idea or concept, then come to a hypothesis according to the dictates of their own minds. The only outside influence entertained as possibly valid is another philosopher's mental speculation that fits the same logic. Therefore, this platform of consciousness, as with the sensual platform, is solely of this world. Scientists and philosophers are attempting to understand everything in this universe or beyond, using only their limited experiences here on earth and whatever speculations come to their minds not of their experience. The material self, mind and body, is considered the "all in all".

The third level of consciousness is the transcendental platform. Only by aspiration for consciousness on this level can the secrets of life, here and beyond, be revealed. This is the platform on which man realizes he is eternal, a spiritual entity that inhabits this body for some time, then leaves it for another to further advance on the spiritual path. A seeker must adopt real spiritual practice to attain this platform of consciousness. On this level man sees with equal vision. He sees all others as spiritual beings covered by different degrees of ignorance from their contact with the material energy. The qualities of goodness begin to be prevalent in the personality. Compassion for other living entities grows within the heart and, not only is he less judgmental towards other people, but there is compassion for the poor defenceless living entities who, by instinct, dwell on the platform of sensuality. A true transcendentalist will no more contribute to the unnecessary slaughter of animals than they would engage in cannibalism to satisfy the palate. When a seeker begins to see the world with spiritual vision, he begins to see God in everyone and everything. Instead of excessive lust, greed and avarice, he begins to feel love and compassion for all. On this platform begins the life of the heart, showing the true goals of human life and the futility of attempting to fashion a permanent home here becomes apparent. while demands of the body and life here must be met, this is not the best use of our advanced intelligence.

We need to ask the most important questions of "who am I?, how did I get here?, who is God?, what is my relationship with God?, and what is the way of transcendence?". Once beginning this quest on the intellectual platform the seekers can raise their consciousness to the spiritual or transcendental platform through practice, only they need to learn how. What can we do to connect with the supreme energy? How to transcend this bodily platform and attain permanent satisfaction and happiness that does not die along with the body? How can we attain peace of mind......freedom from anxiety in our lives?

The secret is explained in the Vedas of ancient India. These texts are the oldest known to man and contain knowledge in the sciences of this world as well as beyond. The most important part of the vedas give explanations of the nature of the soul. There is knowledge of God and the process of realizing our connection to God. The practice of yoga teaches about the body, mind, spirit and how to correlate all three to attain spiritual consciousness. Yoga means to "link up" with the Supreme or God.

In ancient times yogis had to perform many austerities to reach transcendental consciousness. They learned, over many years of practice, how to control prana, the life airs of the body, to attain the spiritual goals. This was done through physical processes and the yogi would also control the mind, going into meditative trance.

Today it is all but impossible to perfect this type of yoga system. There are incredible benefits to practicing hatha yoga, physically, mentally and spiritually, but the meditative state is of the utmost importance. In this age our lifespans are not very long, less than 100 years and our minds are as impossible to control as trying to control the wind. Some advancement can be made, but perfection is not possible without "mantra" meditation. A mantra transcendental sound vibration such as, "Om Narayanaya namaha";... "Om Shivaya namaha";... "Aum";... "Hare Krishna";... etc. is described in the vedas as having the potency to raise the mind's consciousness to the transcendental platform. By finding a quiet place to meditate and repeating a bona-fide mantra, coming from the transcendental stratosphere, some degree of self-realization can start to be achieved, providing the answers to the mysteries of life and the true goals of human life.

One most important thing to be noted is that it's essential to find a teacher who has sufficient knowledge and spiritual realization to help you on this path to transcendence. Supersoul, an expansion of the supreme, is in the heart of all. By beginning spiritual meditation, he or she turns within. Any false ego is shed and there is a connection with the spiritual energy of the universal creation.

A great change begins to take place within your heart when you start this process. You begin to wish good on others, rather than being envious of them for their accomplishments. You begin to feel satisfied and anxiety free, understanding that everything is as it should be. You should do everything possible to attain your goals in life, but not to be unduly worried about the result. You must act, then leave the results up to providence. By learning how to uncover your dormant spiritual consciousness you learn a previously unknown sense of peace of mind, a sense which constantly grows, independent of any material conditions.

I urge each and every one to begin some effort today to gain real peace through raising yourself to the transcendental platform. Do it for your REAL self, that eternal part of you that will never perish. When the power of real love permeates your being, you will know lasting happiness. Knowledge is light and ignorance is darkness. Stand in the light and the problems of this world will shrink to no more than "water in the hoofprint of a calf".*

*Quote from A.C. Bhaktivedanta Swami in a personal letter to the author.

Venus

THE PRACTICALITY OF ASTROLOGY

The use of an astrological horoscope is meant to be practical, not something that seems mystical and obscure. It is meant to be a tool for the accomplishment of life's duties and goals in the most advantageous manner. I have already earlier likened a horoscope to a detailed road-map for life.

The reading you get from an astrologer, as well as your own further delving into the chart and introspection of its meanings, should have a practical basis. You want to be able to make fewer mistakes and better choices, in all areas of life. You can gain better health physically, mentally and spiritually, thus better enabling you to guide yourself on your own life journey.

I always stress that if an astrologer themselves seems to be greatly lacking in physical health, mental peace and the spiritual knowledge known to be based on a bona-fide source, they are not capable of being of any help to anyone else. "Physician heal thyself" is a well used, but true, cliche.

You don't want some mystical sounding reading full of things having no bearing on your present situation, nor your future, in this lifetime and beyond. I have heard of astrologers giving all sorts of supposed "information" on many of a person's past lives and activities. This is generally not possible. Even the most advanced astrologer cannot understand further than one previous life and, even then, not in totality. Much of this "information" is absolutely impossible to substantiate by any accepted ancient texts on the subject and even if you think it valid, what purpose does it serve?

In vedic astrology we look at certain areas of the chart to understand the preceding lifetime and the resultant natural direction of the next life, depending on how activities in the present life affect it. Further than this is pure conjecture and basically is useless to have any bearing on this life, even if it had some validity.

We need to learn to live in the present and astrology should be used to help us make our present more successful, enjoyable and rewarding. You cannot enjoy life unless you learn to "be here now". Think about this for a moment. If we are always worrying about the past, thinking it to have made the present unfulfilling, it does just that. We must deal with how we have acted in the past, but it should be to learn from it and move on. Learn from your mistakes, then don't repeat them. To always be dwelling on the past will keep you from experiencing happiness in the present, or future times. Live, learn and use your knowledge for proper and rightful action.

By the same token we should not always be living in the future. Astrology will show us our destiny and help us to set a proper course in life. With more complete knowledge of ourselves physically, emotionally and spiritually, we are able to perform the right actions to obtain the desired results. This is a fact but we shouldn't always be thinking of the future. Make plans, goals and vows to achieve success in all spheres of life. This takes careful consideration of the future, in this life as well as the next. Be careful not to constantly think of tomorrow, next week, next month, next year, etc. If you do then you cannot be peaceful today. Put concentration on appreciating the world around you, stopping to "smell the roses". In all that you feel, say and do, try to develop character and higher qualities.

Human beings are meant to gain the advanced qualities of cleanliness of mind and body, truth, compassion, fairness, equanimity of mind, kindness, charity, nonviolence, etc. leading to the ability to love. Real love is unconditional, not simply give and take. An astrologer's duty is to help a person understand themselves better in all ways, allowing practical activities to be undertaken to achieve real success, in all things. A reading should leave you feeling enlivened, determined to advance toward desired goals, in a rightful and honest way. You should have been given realistic and practical methods to gain in knowledge and skills to act in knowledge thereby insuring ultimate success.

Your reading of the birth chart should enable you to enact a "rebirth" of sorts, allowing you to take the right directions and actions, from that day forth. When I hear someone say that they've had their birth chart done numerous times, it's obvious they did not get what they should have. We do yearly updates for clients, and other specialized types of astrological services, but one birth chart should be all you need in a lifetime to get the knowledge and direction for maximum enjoyment of life, in all circumstances. Naturally, yearly charts can provide more detail and there are other more specific readings, as already mentioned, such as compatibility charts but, if a life chart has been done properly, it is final. Getting another one done should not alter the basic facts - all you are getting is another interpretation.

SUMMARY POINTS OF PART ONE

Before beginning Part 2 on understanding your horoscope, let's review the major points of the first chapter which will also serve as a handy reference guide.

PHYSICAL HEALTH

1) Astrology can foresee probable ailments and weaknesses. To be forewarned is to be prepared and allows the situation to be avoided or reduced.
2) Karma, the law of action and reaction, is the sum total of all our actions in a particular lifetime and directly creates the destiny for the future life.
3) Look at your diet (a vegetarian diet is the only choice for maintaining proper health), environment, and type of work you do. Avoid processed, convenience foods.
4) Sleep and rest as is necessary according to your age and circumstances.
5) Exercise the body—Do something!! (Hatha yoga is also recommended in the section on "Consciousness and Spirituality").

MENTAL, EMOTIONAL AND SPIRITUAL HEALTH

1) Our true nature is spiritual. Learn the truth. Ignorance and fear create negative emotions, stress, and bewilderment.
2) Understanding reincarnation, or transmigration of the soul, shows us the absurdity of narrowminded "nationalistic" or "racist" arguments.
3) Hate and greed are the most blinding of emotions.
4) The present materialistic attitude prevailing in the world is but an illusion.
5) Our actions will harvest our next rebirth. As you sow, so shall you reap. Action shapes destiny!
6) Unconditional, transcending love is the only way forward.
7) Depression is caused by an ignorance of our true nature and purpose. Spiritual recognition brings hope, understanding, and sense of real purpose in life.
8) Astrology identifies what our true actions should be individually. It arouses interest in and awareness of the spiritual realities of life.
9) Learn to balance physical, mental (including emotional), and spiritual health needs.
10) Try to find a good spiritual teacher/ Get a lifetime horoscope done by a bonafide vedic astrologer. Study it and follow its guidance. Go with life's flow and learn from your mistakes.
11) Learn to love yourself, your neighbour, ultimately the world and all of life. Smile and help make the world a better place. Spread love, not anger and hatred.

RELATIONSHIP COMPATIBILITY

1) Get individual life charts done and interpreted.
2) Try to ensure basic compatibility before commitment to a permanent relationship. Make sure there is a basis of love and affection.
3) Learn about each others qualities and attributes.
4) Learn to communicate and how to listen.
5) Control temper and speaking without thinking—your partner may forgive but won't forget.

HUMAN SEXUALITY

1) Previous incarnations and the karmic balance cause the current bodily form.
2) The changing world and roles have caused a need for changes in the sex role-play of each gender. Women are forced to be more independent to survive. Men have conversely embraced some of the emotional traits of women. The gender gap has become narrower and blurred.

DISCOVERING POTENTIAL AND CHOOSING A CAREER

1) An astrological horoscope will indicate strengths, weaknesses, and propensities which, if acknowledged and utilized, will lead to success.
2) Positive thinking helps along the chosen path.
3) Choose something you enjoy. You should also find that you are successful as a natural consequence.
4) The earlier in life a person receives guidance, the less frustrating will be career advancement. In the east parents automatically get charts prepared for their children at birth. An early start in the right direction cannot be overemphasised. Western parents should give similar thought to this guidance for their children.

PROSPERITY AND POSITIVE THINKING

1) Prosperity is not defined as material success and wealth building. It is a feeling of happiness and satisfaction with life. It comes from spiritual development and self-realization and is built by development of our loving propensity.
2) Whatever you desire you must plan for and dedicate yourself to achieving. Nothing comes without expending effort except for a very few who are reaping the rewards of extreme piety and righteous activity in past lives.
3) You must believe in yourself and what you wish to achieve. Without such positive thought patterns, success of any significance is unlikely.
4) Learn to plan. Write down short and long term goals, then dedicate and discipline yourself to achieve them.
5) Wish love, peace and prosperity to all. "The power of love is a curious thing". (Opening line from the movie theme "Back to the Future".)

CONSCIOUSNESS AND SPIRITUALITY

1) Three levels of consciousness exist—Sensual (experienced also by the animal kingdom); Intellectual— the beginning of philosophical and material questioning; Transcendental — the realization of eternal spiritual growth.
2) Seekers of wisdom and truth (on intellectual platform) must adopt real spiritual practice to attain to and progress beyond this level of consciousness.
3) The practices of yoga and meditation (especially mantra meditation) are recommended.

THE PRACTICALITY OF ASTROLOGY

1) A Roadmap to Life— Make fewer mistakes, take less wrong turnings, be aware of what is ahead of you and where you have come from.

2) Make sure you have confidence in a chosen astrologer. Ensure all the features of the horoscope are explained clearly.
3) Learn to live in and benefit from the present—"Stop to smell the roses".
4) Try to develop good character and higher qualities within yourself, especially truthfulness, compassion, charity, and nonviolence toward all creatures.
5) Only one life chart should be necessary. Annual "yearly" charts provide a detailed map to the immediate part of your journey in this lifetime.
6) No matter what your physical age it is never too late to make improvement and progress in life.

Saturn

PART TWO

UNDERSTANDING THE HOROSCOPE

Rahu

THE PLANETS, SIGNS, AND HOUSES

THE PLANETS:-

In Vedic astrology we are concerned with nine planets. They are the seven planets Sun, Moon, Mars, Mercury, Jupiter, Venus and Saturn, as well as the north and south nodes of the moon, which are mathematical points, actually considered to be shadow planets. Their names are Rahu (the north node, known as Dragon's Head by astronomers) and Ketu (the south node, known as Dragon's Tail). The planets represent the various energies in life. I will give a short description as to the energies represented by the planets, as well as the categories of life which they control. These descriptions are, in an introductory book, necessarily incomplete but will give an understanding of the basics of what the planets represent in the horoscope.

The planets also have natures described as benefic (giving or good) or malefic (troublesome or bad). These can be altered by:-
    a) conjunctions (other planets they are with in the same house),
    b) aspects by other planets (to be discussed later,)
    c) the houses they rule according to the rising sign (also to be discussed later,).

The natural effects of Jupiter, Venus, Moon and Mercury are said to be benefic, although the Moon and Mercury can easily be adversely affected by conjunction with malefic planets. Mars, Saturn, Sun, Rahu and Ketu are said to be natural malefics. The Sun is considered a malefic, due to the fact of its great heat and ability to consume.

SUN

Of primary importance is the Sun's representation of the soul, or "real" self and the level of awareness as to this knowledge of spirit soul.

The Sun also represents the external, physical appearance of a person. It will indicate the health and stature of the body as well as physical beauty. It will be an indicator of what types of behaviour, or actions, an individual is likely to engage in and the quality of the engagement. Additionally, the Sun is representative of a person's father in this life.

The Sun will show whether or not you are meant to lead, or are best suited to a position of assisting. It will also indicate whether you are more adept to working in groups, or alone. Influence, fame (or infamy) and popularity are other factors of the Sun's position.

MOON

The Moon represents the mind and how you think, feel and the level of self motivation. It is indicative of the basic mental condition or emotional health. It will show quality of emotions and sensitivity. Much can be gleaned of a person's capability for action, in both words and deeds, by the position of the Moon.

The Moon rules over all bodies of water, such as the seas, as well as liquids in general, including the watery substances (blood, etc.) within the body. Affairs related to an individual's mother are indicated and it can represent women in general. It is concerned with business activity and dealings with the public. It indicates health as a child or teenager.

MARS

Mars is the planet which represents our physical energy, strength and whether we utilize our energy positively or negatively in life. It will indicate courage or fearlessness and determination to succeed in all endeavours. It will also indicate levels of passion, including sexual.

Mars rules over all competitive activities, including sports and military activities. It will even point to what affinity exists in cooking food or succeeding in the restaurant business. It has jurisdiction over business affairs concerning properties (real estate) and automobiles, or other types of machinery. The position of Mars may also indicate happenings concerning brothers, when appropriate.

MERCURY

Mercury is best known as the planet ruling over communication, of all types, throughout the world. As such, it is representative of intellect as well as the level of education and knowledge you are capable of attaining. It will indicate whether the talent exists to be a good, convincing speaker or orator. It shows mental ability, agility and and how astute a person may become, especially in business dealings.

The ability to communicate also inter-links with people and relationships. The number of relationships/friendships that will be formed stems from the position of this planet in the chart.

Mercury is the planet ruling the depth of memory and therefore the ability to learn foreign languages, etc.

JUPITER

Jupiter is the most wonderful and giving of all the planets. Primarily it indicates your philosophical and religious nature, the amount of knowledge you can gain and assimilate in this regard together with the ability to devote yourself to spiritual life.

Jupiter indicates the rewards due in this life, such as material wealth, financial stability and how influential you may be over others. It shows capability as a teacher and is the indicator for children. Additionally Jupiter represents the husband in a woman's horoscope.

VENUS

·Venus is also a wonderful and giving planet, ruling over much of the beauty in life as well as it's pleasures. Therefore Venus naturally rules over sensual affairs, or love life. In a man's chart it is representative of the wife. It shows an ability to gain in luxuries and possessions, such as automobiles, jewellry and works of art. It will indicate the level of opulence possible to attain in this life, including the enjoyment of ensuing comforts.

Venus rules all the beautiful things in life, including artistic and musical talent and the enjoyment of these things. To be thought of as an alluring or charismatic person also depends on the position of Venus in the horoscope.

SATURN

Saturn is the slowest moving of the planets and most importantly rules over the speed at which the physical body ages, death and longevity of other things generally. It is the indicator of work or career and, as such, the struggle to succeed at endeavours in this material world. It indicates foreigners, foreign countries and the ability to influence groups of people, whether at home or abroad. Its position at times also shows an affinity for black market or illegal business dealings.

Saturn indicates desire to help unfortunate persons or to engage in social service work. Last, but by no means least, it is known to rule over yoga, mysticism and the desire to ultimately renounce the affairs of this world.

RAHU

Rahu, the north node of the Moon, basically causes problems. It rules over poisons and intoxicants as well as unbecoming inclinations of all kinds. It causes all types of suffering, resulting in great delusion and frustration. It creates fearfulness and is known to give extremely chaotic results during its planetary period. Except in certain circumstances, it has a negative effect on any planet with which it is associated.

KETU

Ketu, the south node of the Moon, is a great teacher but it does so by restricting and constraining activities. Like Rahu, it causes problems, basically afflicting any planet associated with it. It is known to create impediments in the execution of activities, presenting diverse stumbling blocks. It can cause poverty, all kinds of material suffering, or undiagnosable diseases, depending on it's position in the chart.

In a positive light it represents the desire for liberation from material entanglement and the hardships caused may push an individual towards the path of self-realization.

THE SIGNS

The signs give the qualities to the energies represented by the planets. The sky is divided by the zodiacal signs and constellations of stars within them. Mathematically we view the sky as an oval of a total of 360 degrees. Therefore, as there are twelve signs, each covers 30 degrees. The planets move in their respective orbits through the twelve signs at a rate of speed determined by their size and distance from the Sun. The Sun is also seen to move completely through the constellations once in a year but, of course, this is from our perception on earth, as all planets actually orbit the Sun, which is situated at the centre of this solar system.

These descriptions are by no means complete or all-encompassing in themselves and are only to give a general idea of the qualities of the signs.

ARIES

Aries, the first sign, is a fire sign and it is ruled over by the planet Mars. The zodiacal symbol is two rams butting heads. It is a masculine sign and is quite martial, or military, in its qualities. It gives spontaneity and makes for a somewhat adventurous nature. It can give qualities of strength and a competitive spirit.

TAURUS
Taurus is an earth sign and is ruled by the planet Venus. Its zodiacal symbol is the bull, which indicates a stubborn but productive nature. It is a feminine sign and, being ruled by Venus, may give artistic abilities.

GEMINI
Gemini is an air sign and is ruled by the planet Mercury. Its symbol is the pair of twins or lovers, indicating variety in tastes. It may make a subject very attractive to others and give skills and knowledge in many different things. Gemini may also indicate a talkative nature.

CANCER
Cancer is a water sign and is ruled by the Moon. Its symbol is the crab. Generally it gives a sensitive and/or emotional nature which, depending on position, may indicate psychic abilities. It has a spiritual nature, yet its natives may be seen to have strong attachments within this world.

LEO
Leo is a fire sign, ruled by the Sun. Its symbol is the lion, indicating a somewhat martial or "intense" nature. Generally, Leo gives great aspirations and the ability to accomplish many goals in life. It makes for a righteous and upstanding nature and a natural-born leader of others. Leo can give a powerful appearance, physically or in posture, yet with a kind disposition.

VIRGO
Virgo is an earth sign, ruled by Mercury. Its symbol is the virgin, indicating a soft, possibly feminine, nature. It often makes for an artistic inclination and gives a very expressive nature. Virgoans frequently have a good sense of humour and are meticulous individuals.

LIBRA
Libra is an air sign, ruled by the planet Venus. Its symbol is the scales, which suggests a good balance between the spiritual and material sides of life. Librans are usually concerned with other people, honesty or justice deep within and frequently wish to perform activities aimed at helping the underpriveledged or downtrodden. It often indicates the ability to engage in profitable partnerships.

SCORPIO
Scorpio is a water sign, ruled by Mars. Its symbol is the scorpion, which means those under this sign may have a tendency to be critical or even cruel. It may indicate a vengeful nature, although those under this influence generally live anything but boring lives. Excitement, or "living- on-the-edge", may be commonplace at times. This is an extremely spiritual sign, thus the higher nature of Scorpio can lead to the path of transcendence.

SAGITTARIUS

Sagittarius is a fire sign, ruled by the planet Jupiter. Its symbol is the archer, which generally indicates high goals and principles of character. Sagittarians are ambitious people, capable of gaining spiritual understandings and direction in life. It is considered a holy sign, representative of saints and spiritual preceptors.

CAPRICORN

Capricorn is an earth sign, ruled by the planet Saturn. It is symbolized by the crocodile which seems to indicate patience. As it is a slow planet it may indicate a slowness in actions. It gives power and influence for a committed and determined individual. It can give power over, or respect from, the general public.

AQUARIUS

Aquarius is an air sign, also ruled by Saturn. Its symbol is a woman carrying pots, indicating a person who shoulders a great burden or does service for other people. It gives interest in spirituality, mysticism and the occult. It may make individuals appear to be exceedingly eccentric in their methodology of action. Aquarius is most definitely a great teacher, though it is through difficulties that the lessons are learned.

PISCES

Pisces is a water sign, ruled over by the planet Jupiter. Its zodiacal symbol is two fish swimming in opposite directions. This indicates a difficulty in making decisions and a soft, unselfish nature. Being ruled by Jupiter it is a spiritual sign and those under its influence are ultimately concerned with spiritual liberation.

THE HOUSES

Once it is ascertained in which signs the planets were situated at the time of birth, we need to put the signs in the numbered houses. The houses, as they're called, represent the specific applications of activity or the categories of life that the planets, in their signs, are enacting. The way we place them is by first finding the rising or ascendant sign. Whichever sign was due east on the horizon at the time of birth is the rising sign and is placed in the first house. Then all signs go in their natural order. In other words, if Sagittarius is determined to be the rising sign it goes in the first house, along with any planets situated within the sign. Then Capricorn goes in the second house, Aquarius in the third, Pisces in the fourth, etc.

We use what is called an "equal house system" in vedic astrology, which means that if the rising point or ascendant is 10 degrees Sagittarius, the whole sign of Sagittarius goes into the first house. This is true regardless of what degree the rising point is. The entire sign which the rising point falls within is considered the first house. Houses are not set up according to the degree of rising, as in the most common "divided house system" used by many western astrologers today. I will attempt to give some of the categories of life connected with the houses but, again for simplicity's sake in an introductory book, it is not meant to be complete or detailed.

THE FIRST HOUSE
The first house shows the strength of the chart or of this lifetime as a whole. It indicates the types of aspirations and direction that may be taken. It will reflect not only physical appearance, but the health or well-being of the physical nature. It demonstrates the strength of character and how individuals are likely to represent themselves to the world.

THE SECOND HOUSE
The second house is concerned with business generally, the banking of money, gemstones, financial situations and ability for earning a living. It also indicates the face and mouth, thereby the speaking abilities as well as eating tendencies. It also reflects the degree of philosophical nature.

THE THIRD HOUSE
The third house deals with communication. Therefore it rules over speech, type of voice and literary talent. Manual dexterity may also be determined from this house, as well as bravery and determination to achieve goals in life. Brothers also are indicated.

THE FOURTH HOUSE
The fourth house is indicative of heart-felt feelings and emotions, as well as level of education obtained in school environments. It can tell about friends and relationships with your mother. Materially it rules properties and vehicles or machinery, such as cars and the like. It also reflects the living environment that can be expected.

THE FIFTH HOUSE
The fifth house is mostly involved with children but there are many other categories looked at. We can tell the level of intelligence and the level of capacity which exists to become an accomplished student or teacher. It gives an inkling of the previous birth and what spiritual desires may exist. This house also indicates the presence (or absence) of a romantic nature and level of social interaction. It is looked to for ability to profit from financial investments and the entertainment industry.

THE SIXTH HOUSE
The sixth house is often called the "house of diseases, or troubles". We can tell the susceptibility to disease as well as the possible types of ailments you may have problems with. It also indicates troubles from enemies in life and financial debts. It reflects uncles, foreigners and foreign travels, the ability to serve others, service to God and worship at churches, temples, mosques, synagogues, etc.

THE SEVENTH HOUSE
The seventh house is most commonly referred to as the "marriage and relationship" house. It shows the success or failure of business relationships or

partnerships as well as marital-type relationships. It rules over short trips you may undertake and certain businesses, especially those having connection with the general public.

THE EIGHTH HOUSE

The eighth house is where we look for longevity of the body or the life span. As such it is sometimes called the "house of death". It indicates various sufferings and unfortunate circumstances. We can understand psychological make-up and psychic or mystical abilities. Physically it rules the anus and the elimination system. It can indicate whether or not there is likely gain from insurance or through inheritance.

THE NINTH HOUSE

The ninth house is considered to be the most important house in the horoscope. It is termed the "house of good fortune". As such it shows what boons may be received in this lifetime. These include meeting a spiritual teacher capable of disseminating spiritual knowledge, religious feelings and general good fortune in all areas of life. It indicates the government or superiors, the father and even grandchildren. It may also demonstrate the ability to earn through the importation, exportation, or shipping of goods.

THE TENTH HOUSE

The tenth house is usually looked to for information on type of career, as well as success and standing within it. It will show the type of engagement to earn money and the ability to be successful in this respect. It also indicates public standing or reputation, family lineage and political leanings.

THE ELEVENTH HOUSE

The eleventh house we usually refer to as the "house of enjoyment or pleasures". It indicates desires in this regard and the degree of success in fulfiling them. It shows opportunities for earning money with little work or effort and also rules over sisters and pets. Without an adequately strong eleventh house it is impossible to attain much material pleasure or satisfaction, regardless of success in career, etc.

THE TWELFTH HOUSE

The twelfth house is known as the "house ruling material losses", but, conversely, shows renunciation of materialism for spiritual benefit. It indicates expenditures of finance and mental confusion, sleep, dreams, sexual pleasures, charitableness toward others, the desire for spiritual liberation and indications as to the next birth may be ascertained from this house. Benefic planets in this house do not generally bode well for material prosperity.

Ketu

THE RISING SIGN

The rising or ascendant sign, is most important in understanding the general personality of an individual. It will indicate a person's drive, goal-orientation and quality of action. The rising sign is determined to be the sign due east on the horizon at the time of birth. It is placed in the first house and all other signs follow in their natural order placed in houses two through to twelve. In other words, if Sagittarius is the rising sign (ascendant) Capricorn would be in the second house, Aquarius in the third, Pisces in the fourth, Aries in the fifth, etc. with Scorpio finally being in the twelfth house. The following are short, general descriptions of the qualities of the various signs when they are rising in the horoscope.

ARIES RISING

These people are of a masculine nature as Aries is ruled by Mars. They are quite dominant, with a tendency to take leadership positions and make good military officers. They can plan things out and direct others to action. They have good ambition, courage and the fortitude to surmount all sorts of problems. They may also show anger if provoked and cannot be intimidated, but will work with others to achieve what they consider of importance. They are proud people, with logical minds.

Aries are travellers and are always on the move. They are usually physically strong, as well as good-looking. Beauty in all things is attractive to them and they prefer to live places where the natural splendour of mother nature is obvious. They have an affinity for spicy food. Exercise is also a part of their lives, although they may experience some weakness of their joints. Success in businesses to do with property, real estate, etc. is indicated.

TAURUS RISING

This is a sign ruled by Venus and people under this sign love beauty in all things. They often have a sensual nature and appearance. Although generally good-looking with a friendly, compassionate personality, when they get mad, "look out!" These people have the fortitude and energy to be successful in their careers and anything else they may desire to accomplish.

They are intelligent, artistic and can be very generous with others. Although rather independent they are extremely capable and get the job done, but may be somewhat of a perfectionist, at times. These people make excellent friends and, while good to their spouses, don't get as much pleasure from children as others may. Their children are mostly female.

GEMINI RISING

This sign is ruled by Mercury which rules over communication of all kinds, from transportation to authors, writers, speakers and researchers, etc. These natives are extremely intelligent but often not consistent in their actions. They make good teachers or preachers and are good in the "nuts and bolts" of running a business, especially keeping track of finance. However, sometimes they take on too many engagements to do well, as they love change and variety.

These people can be very perceptive of other's desires and reasons for doing things. They are good speakers and fast thinkers. They may also be artistic. More often than not they also enjoy full social lives and, due to liking change, they require stimulation or they become bored. Usually they're found in intellectual positions or jobs where they use their brains, rather than their bodies.

CANCER RISING

This sign is ruled by the Moon. As the Moon represents the mind and emotions, they can be easily upset. Often they don't feel like others are appreciative of them and may tend to voice their sensitivities in this regard. They do have a good nature and care for people in their lives. They enjoy their homes and all that they possess. As long as they have what they need, they tend to be happy. They are friendly and their interests are myriad.

Being a water sign, Cancerians like to live near the water and also love foreign travel. They love their families and friends and enjoy their company a great deal. They are communicators and may be in business where contact with the general public is predominant. They are not usually interested in having a large family, although they are somewhat dependent on their marriage partners to make them feel they are cared for.

LEO RISING

Ruled by the Sun, these people often become famous or well-known, achieve power and high positions by dint of their sheer force and great energy. A born leader who doesn't like to be bossed around. Very large or powerful looking physically and may be intimidating to others, due to their outspoken nature. They are brave, sincere, friendly to others, affectionate, attractive and have good hearts.

They set high goals for themselves and may work tirelessly toward these ends. They are extremely independent and forceful in their opinions but are kind and honourable people. They are honest in their dealings and sincere in words and deeds. They like the outdoors and natural beauty. Due to their nature, they may be difficult to live with, resulting in more than one marriage. They tend to be successful materially, due to their energy, in all they undertake and have spiritual interest.

VIRGO RISING

This sign is ruled over by the planet Mercury. These are pleasant people with good intelligence and a soft heart. They may be creative and artistic, with varied interests in life, deep thinkers, as well as very capable in their careers and businesses. They are philosophical and only do things that they feel good about, although at times they may be too impulsive.

These people love beauty and the pure riches of mother earth. They have good discretion most of the time and are able to work for things they wish to accomplish. They prefer variety in their occupations and in life in general, lest they become tired of what they are doing. In general these are lovely people that care about others but are not always sure of themselves. They have good habits and are well liked by others around them.

LIBRA RISING

This sign is under the rulership of Venus giving a love of art, beauty and the good things of life. Those affected are adept at balancing the different sides of human life. They have a love for other people and are helped by friends and family. They are talented in business and have desires to make themselves an asset to the masses of people by their actions. They possess good intellectual capabilities and are good at dealing impartially with other people, although they may be quite opinionated.

They have an affinity for sensual pleasures and prefer an opulent environment. Honest, with good discretion, more often than not they are tall and slender, with light skin and hair. They are fun-loving and helpful to those close to them. They are usually philosophical or religious and care sincerely for others, taking compassion on those less fortunate in life.

SCORPIO RISING

This is the sign ruled by Mars and problematic childhood is not uncommon. Usually they are good looking with a dark complexion. They are very demanding, intense people more often than not and can have a cruel streak, especially if someone has wronged them. They have the energy to accomplish their aims and are very opinionated. They have good intelligence and are usually talented in what they do. They care for others and give of themselves when they feel appreciated.

Artistic and good communicators, they have problems in marriage, due to their temperament and anger. Often these people are hard to read, somewhat mysterious and yet are capable of greatness, as well as lowly acts. They definitely have spiritual inclinations.

SAGITTARIUS RISING

Sagittarius is ruled by the planet Jupiter. These people are honest, energetic and straightforward people who are generally high achievers or goal-setters. They are principled people, generally full of good qualities who want justice to reign and have the ability to counsel or teach others. They have good mental and physical health for the most part and usually are spiritually inclined. These people don't like hypocrites and they are very philosophical about life.

Usually tall, with a longish face, large nose and brownish hair, they are excellent business people and can use their power over others wisely. They tend to prevail over those that oppose them yet, generally, are more successful far from their places of birth. They have good intelligence and absorb spiritual teachings that they can impart to others. They may suffer from the envy of others but, in general, are respected and live fulfiling lives.

CAPRICORN RISING

Capricorn is ruled by the planet Saturn. Those born under this ascendant are liked by others, although they tend to put their own desires first and foremost. They persevere and, generally, set high goals for themselves. Although they may seem negative they can attain greatness, power and fame, achieving things difficult to obtain by the average person. They do exercise patience in working toward their desires until they are realized. They are multi-talented and may change their mode of employment, liking the variety. This also makes them enjoy travel. Physically they may be thin and good-looking, with sandy or brownish hair. They are successful in business for they will do whatever they feel is necessary to achieve their goals, even to the point of underhandedness at times. In marriage they often choose someone senior in age and don't usually have many children.

AQUARIUS RISING

The sign Aquarius is under the rulership of the planet Saturn. These people are generally good communicators, have intelligent ideas and may be found teaching. Others are generally fond of these folks. They are quite philosophical and many people have difficulty understanding them. They like to help others and are good natured. Frequently, their health is weak. Many times these people feel insecure in marriage or their relations with the opposite sex, although they enjoy an active social life.

They like the outdoors and beautiful places. Generally they don't wish to be in positions of authority, although they will work hard at whatever task they are given. They are interested in ancient cultures and sometimes in religion or the occult. They may not always be the most generous people but are friendly, well-liked, possessing intelligence and foresight.

PISCES RISING

This sign is ruled over by the planet Jupiter. Those born under its influence make good marital partners, yet may be distrusting of their partners and their actions. They have a lot of energy to achieve results and may be very successful, with great influence. They are adept with finance and they are sometimes found in the world of high finance or in the entertainment world.

They are honest people, with an interest in spiritual things. They may have psychic abilities but often have a hard time making up their minds. They love to travel overseas. Fond of romance, they are kind and may be an inspiration to others. They are sensual and, although quite advanced in many things, often their minds are not at peace.

PLANETS IN THE SIGNS AND HOUSES

In this section are descriptions of the possible effects of the planets when situated in specific signs and houses. Planets are powerful when in their own signs, the signs they rule over or are lord of. They are even more powerful when in their exaltation signs. Furthermore, planets have inter-relationships as friends or enemies, as do people. As a result of this their influences are stronger when with friends than in the signs of enemies and worst in their signs of debilitation.

To understand this we first must know which signs planets rule and what is their exaltation and debilitation signs. Information as to enemy's or friend's signs is contained in the individual descriptions but a listing of rulership, exaltation and debilitation signs follows:

SUN = Ruler of Leo /Exalted in Aries /Debilitated in Libra

MOON = Ruler of Cancer /Exalted in Taurus /Debilitated in Scorpio

MARS = Ruler of Aries & Scorpio /Exalted in Capricorn /Debilitated in Cancer

MERCURY = Ruler of Gemini & Virgo /Exalted in Virgo /Debilitated in Pisces

JUPITER = Ruler Sagittarius & Pisces / Exalted in Cancer / Debilitated in Capricorn

VENUS = Ruler of Taurus & Libra / Exalted in Pisces / Debilitated in Virgo

SATURN = Ruler of Capricorn & Aquarius / Exalted in Libra / Debilitated in Aries

Rahu and Ketu are shadow planets and, as such, they really can't own any particular sign. However they do exercise a successful bearing, when in certain signs. They also have exaltation and debilitation signs, as follows:-

RAHU = Strong in Virgo, stronger in Aquarius /exalted in Taurus /debilitated in Scorpio

KETU = Strong in Pisces, stronger in Leo / exalted in Scorpio /debilitated in Taurus

Another thing to be noted is that Rahu and Ketu are said to act rather like the lords of the signs they are in. Therefore, if Rahu or Ketu is in Capricorn, look to the strength of position of Saturn and predict effects accordingly. If in Pisces, look to Jupiter, etc.

Now we will look at the individual planets and general effects of their being situated in specific signs and houses within the horoscope.

NB. There are situations that will give cancellation of debilitation. One such situation is if the debilitated planet is in the first, fourth, seventh, or tenth house from the ascendant sign, or the Moon.

Other situations are:
(a) If the ruler of the sign where the debilitated planet is situated is in the first, fourth, seventh, or tenth house from the ascendant or Moon.

(b) If the planet which becomes exalted in the sign which the debilitated planet is situated is in the first, fourth, seventh, or tenth house from the ascendant or Moon.

(c) If the planet in debilitation is exalted in the "Navamsa" chart, there is cancellation of debilitation. (Navamsa chart is the most important "subdivisional" chart in Vedic astrology. Subdivisionals will be discussed later)

SUN IN ARIES

This is the most powerful sign for the Sun to be situated. It is the sign ruled by the planet Mars. Those thus influenced are generally powerful people, both in mind and body, as well as in spirit. These are people that feel born to lead. They usually have good discretion and ideas for material, as well as spiritual, advancement. Goal setters, extremely competitive and quite intelligent, they are unforgettable personalities. They're not afraid to get involved and sometimes they may push themselves too hard. They may earn great wealth, yet, at times, not have much more than they need to keep body and soul together. These people like to travel and may become well known.

SUN IN TAURUS

This sign is ruled by the planet Venus which makes these people sensual, loving beauty both in things generally and the environment in particular. They are very "down to earth", practical people. These people are dependable, have ambition and can work steadily in their time to achieve their goals. They are very strong willed and can be extremely stubborn at times. Making them angry will never get them to concede, so it's wise to be kind and patient.

These people are fairly analytical and don't rush into things without thinking. They have high intelligence, patience and believe in themselves and their abilities. They can be very talented in business and usually marry well. They enjoy food and may have musical talents.

SUN IN GEMINI

This is a sign ruled by the planet Mercury. These very intelligent people have capable abilities in many different areas, especially the sciences of life and are usually well educated. These are successful persons who are skillful with money and do well in their careers. They are polite, kind to others and are extremely good communicators. Talented in many things, sometimes they tend to try to do too much at once and can become tired from the endeavour.

They are loving people and are talented in the art of love making. These are social people who require much variety in life, lest they become bored. There is always so much going on with them that they are very interesting but frequently have the tendency to moodiness.

SUN IN CANCER

This is the sign ruled by the Moon. These people are honest, usually quite emotional and like to live in places near the ocean, lakes, rivers, etc. They spend a great deal of time at home and are usually happy there yet, they also like travelling to foreign countries and enjoy warm weather.

These are people that have good discretion and may do things according to what their "sixth sense" tells them is right. They may be somewhat on the conservative side and are very sincere in their love for others. Generally they are successful and may become rich but they also have experience of hard times in life. They can see the reality in things and can give good instruction or advice. They love to enjoy themselves but, on the health side, may have stomach problems and should be aware of this aspect.

SUN IN LEO

This is the sign ruled by the Sun, therefore it is powerful in this position. These people are generally physically strong, good-looking, with lots of energy and can become very successful in their career and many other things that they set out to do. They are egotistical, headstrong and sometimes may be considered too intense. In marriage they often have problems because they think that they are always right, although actually, they often are.

This position also means that there is some assistance from their father or from authorities in life. They have high goals and are good communicators. Most people like and are willing to help them. They are sincere and can be quite influential over others. Having the intelligence and the drive to accomplish their objectives, they invariably do. They are not usually much troubled by sickness and love the great outdoors. Natural scenery is what they enjoy best and they may go out alone to think or meditate. These people are also philosophical and are often learned in spiritual subjects.

SUN IN VIRGO

This sign is ruled by the planet Mercury and gives many positive qualities. Those influenced are kind, unimposing people with intellect and a substantial education. They are excellent communicators and may be very artistic. They have discretion and are creative in their approach to things. Attractive people, with an innocence about them, these persons are open, honest and care sincerely for others. Although others like to be around them for their sincerity, occasionally they can be too forceful in their opinions. Physically they are not very strong or powerful. In general these people are full of talents, but they can be a little weak, mentally, in perseverance. They can be very successful in their career or in business for they take care of even the little things that others may not recognize as being important.

SUN IN LIBRA

This sign is ruled by Venus and is the weakest sign to have the Sun in the birth chart. Those influenced, although good in business, are better suited working with other people and not independently. They are usually straightforward, fair and honest in their opinions and dealings. They care and will do things for others. They can be generous but are often misunderstood. These people are sensually inclined and like beautiful things. They abhor violence and like life to be full of harmony and love. However, they aren't always very moralistic and should beware of associating with others that may drag them down. Physically they may have poor eyesight, stomach problems and headaches.

SUN IN SCORPIO

This sign is ruled by Mars. Those in this situation are good-looking people with "action-packed" lives. They may hide their thoughts and actions and may do things without first considering the implications. They are fighters and may like firearms or other types of weapons. They are determined and work toward their goals. They may not be trusting of others and the same may be true of others' feelings toward them, often being, justifiably, thought of as devious. They can be nervous and have a sharp tongue. These people do have aspirations to help humanity at large and may be involved with groups that they believe can work for the ultimate good of the country or the world. They are capable and can be successful in their careers, which often include becoming teachers, musicians, or, doing work in the medical professions or real estate.

SUN IN SAGITTARIUS

This sign is ruled by Jupiter which gives many endearing qualities to those influenced. They are generally honest, reliable and straightforward. They set themselves high goals and work toward their fruition. Other people believe and put faith in them. They are, more often than not, philosophical, religious, optimistic and like to live good clean lives.

They are capable people that achieve success and often become rich. They have keen discretion and are generous, kind and fair, but may be lacking in patience. Generally the physical health is pretty reliable and they have strong minds. These are people that can be depended on and make very reliable friends, able to offer sound advice.

SUN IN CAPRICORN

This sign is ruled by the planet Saturn. Those in this position are intelligent and may have great ideas but don't like to be rushed. "Slow but sure" is an accurate description. They are capable in business and generally good with maths. They are extremely independent, like to rely on their own ways of doing things and don't like to be told what to do.

These are not the most optimistic people in the world and often are interested in philosophical concepts beyond the here and now. These people may get into important positions by perseverance, or may have associates that are in elevated positions. They are honest, compassionate towards others, have a sharp sense of humour and are not generally loud or boisterous, indeed, usually quite the opposite.

SUN IN AQUARIUS

This sign is ruled by the planet Saturn. These people are intelligent communicators and make excellent writers. They are dependable, fast learners and do whatever is necessary to get their jobs finished properly. They experience ups and downs in career and their financial position. Often they find in their jobs that they have to listen to people that are not nearly as capable as they are. Their minds are always active and can come up with good ideas for other people's benefit, gaining respect and love. Usually they are taught spiritual or philosophical concepts just by dint of the setbacks they undergo in life.

SUN IN PISCES

This sign is ruled by the planet Jupiter and, as a result, these people are usually interested in philosophy and religion. They are kind and loving people that will almost always help another. They are usually good-looking people but may be somewhat introverted, especially with strangers. They like to be near the water and enjoy a beautiful environment. These people are well liked, intelligent and have soft personalities. Sometimes they are taken advantage of.

They like others but need to develop more confidence in themselves. They treat people with respect and are appreciated by the opposite gender. They have strong discretion and usually have a steady marriage that helps them go further in life. Physically they may gain weight easily and have digestive problems.

SUN IN FIRST HOUSE

This is a powerful and independent person who likes to be the centre of attention. They are extremely capable but may be a little egotistical. However they are well intentioned, honest and brave. They are attractive but may have poor vision. They enjoy travelling and seeing all sorts of things. These are successful people who set high goals and have the ingenuity and energy to accomplish them. They have the ability to give direction to, but don't like to be directed by, others. They like to socialize, but also appreciate their privacy.

Not only are they successful in material things, but they also have a philosophical nature and a desire to understand spiritual subject matters. They may attain a high position in life and become well known. Their spouse must defer to their wishes, usually, or there are problems.

SUN IN SECOND HOUSE

This is a powerful person, not only physically, but in character. They are intelligent and usually have a substantial education. They may be a bit hard-headed and have problems resulting from opposing their superiors. They are eloquent speakers and reliable workers. They usually have adequate finances, but aren't usually wealthy. Their father and mother are fond of them and often give them monetary assistance. They may have problems with their teeth.

SUN IN THIRD HOUSE

This is an excellent placement. These people are intelligent and very expressive. They are of a strong physical constitution and are brave and determined. Usually they have agreeable parents. Energetic, kind to others and well liked, these people are known to be very ingenious.

SUN IN FOURTH HOUSE

These are very affable people that have a keen intellect. There may have been breaks in their education, but they are sufficiently knowledgeable. They usually own property or homes and although they establish relationships with people of high standing, very few people know them intimately. They like to work in or on things in which they believe.

SUN IN FIFTH HOUSE

These are people that rise to elevated positions in life. Generally they are good-looking, with a sound physical constitution. They may visit many different places and like to enjoy themselves. Often they become teachers.They may have digestive problems.

SUN IN SIXTH HOUSE

These may be powerful people of a strong physical constitution. They generally prevail over those with whom they have problems. They like to visit other countries and have interest in how other people live and work. They frequently work with lawyers or doctors and may become well known.

SUN IN SEVENTH HOUSE

These are capable people that have difficulty listening to the advice of others. They generally are entrepreneurs and can manage their businesses well. They sometimes have problems in marriage as they are hard to get close to in relationships. They sometimes become well known.

SUN IN EIGHTH HOUSE

These people have some philosophical inclinations and don't usually hanker to be the centre of attention. They have small families and may work for the state. Usually they live a great distance from where they were born. Physically they may have stomach problems and poor vision.

SUN IN NINTH HOUSE

These are people that achieve in life. They have great goals and are excellent communicators. They are quite "intense" and may be leaders with great influence. Their love lives are usually problematic. They may be travellers or deal in import and export businesses.

SUN IN TENTH HOUSE

These are very capable, intelligent, people that care for others and are very helpful to those less fortunate. They make ideal leaders and like to talk. They are quite sensually inclined as well as having a strong physical constitution.

SUN IN ELEVENTH HOUSE

These people may be very successful in their career and can accumulate many possessions. They do not have many close friends and need to develop more generosity toward others.

SUN IN TWELFTH HOUSE

These people are generally philosophically inclined and don't have much drive for advancement in the career. They enjoy travelling and may not stay in any one job for very long. They may have poor vision and their father may leave when they are quite young.

MOON IN ARIES

Aries is a sign ruled over by Mars. It makes for physically powerful people with good health and a love for action. They are outgoing, aggressive, exciting people who may be intimidating to others. Country life is not to their liking as there is not enough to do to keep them busy. They have high opinions of themselves and feel capable of almost anything, which is often the truth.

They are sexual people and usually talented in love making. People like them and generally they have many friends. They are often property owners and may become wealthy through their efforts in their career. They are usually the eldest child of the family. Physically they may suffer from headaches, respiratory problems or weak teeth.

MOON IN TAURUS

This is a sign ruled by Venus and is the most powerful sign for the Moon, making for strong mental faculties. Those so affected love beauty, art, nature and may be very sensual. They are resolute in their motives and generally know exactly what they want and how to attain it. They are usually honest, moralistic and learn good traits from their mother. Serious about things they believe in, they often become angry if provoked and have a stubborn nature.

They enjoy food and may have a tendency to put on weight. They don't like to be hurried or pushed but take their time, being careful in their actions. These are influential people and are generous to those close to them. They have high intelligence and keen discretion. They can be extremely tolerant and discerning of others.

MOON IN GEMINI

This sign is ruled by Mercury, indicating an intelligent person with a love for many things, especially art, music, beautiful clothing and jewellry. They are quick learners, excellent communicators, successful in speaking and in business dealings. They are such good speakers that it is common to find them in the communications business. They can do more than one thing at one time and often do so. They may have more than one occupation and also more than one spouse throughout their life. They are perceptive, discerning of intentions, non-violent and usually successful people.

MOON IN CANCER

Cancer is ruled by the Moon, indicating a powerful mind. It is a water sign so these people like living near the water and find business successes in watery products, or related things, such as pearls,etc. They are emotional people and may be offended by harshness, accordingly they are usually caring for the feelings of others. Philosophical about life they take things in their stride, maintaining a placid attitude. Harsh speech will not stir them to action, only kindness. They have loving mothers who are important to them and instill good traits in their personalities when young.

They enjoy and can give many pleasures in life. They are of a strong physical constitution and determined mentally. They like home life and all that goes with it but often have several marriages. They may take shelter in drinking or some such thing at times, to calm the mind. They have reliable friends, possibly in high positions and are generally happy people.

MOON IN LEO

This is the sign ruled by the Sun and people with the influence of Moon here usually are positive and determined. They feel "born to lead others" and can be demanding and somewhat self-centred. Although they are fair, discrete and righteous persons, once they are intent on something, nothing or nobody can usually change their mind. Their associates are rich and often have high positions.

They are outspoken, confident and not bothered by public opinion. They may get angry, without much provocation and can be extremely emotional, which may affect their judgement but will calm down and forget it just as quickly. This is a generous, courageous person who fights for beliefs but, as the Moon represents the mind, there may be mental inebriety, due to so much powerful energy there.

MOON IN VIRGO

This sign is ruled over by Mercury, which generally makes for a good communicator, talented in business dealings. They can understand others as well as make themselves understood. These are caring people that do have feelings for others. They like nature and natural beauty. This sign generally makes individuals attractive with beautiful eyes.

They have high intelligence and can be calculative and quick. They may seem to be somewhat eccentric to some but they articulate well, making people feel at ease. They like sensual relationships with the opposite sex but often seem detached. Their children will be mostly female.

MOON IN LIBRA

This is a sign ruled by Venus, which results in desires for sensual, beautiful things. They are sexually active and often overindulgent, which can, at times, cause them health problems. They are intelligent people, with strong perceptions and discretion. They strike a fair balance between material life and the spiritual side.

Generally happy, nonenvious people, they are respectful of others and do not like to be involved in arguments. They succeed in business, especially partnerships and are honest in their dealings. Popular, they enjoy an active social life and have a special affinity with art and music.

MOON IN SCORPIO

This sign is ruled by Mars but this is the weakest sign for the Moon, resulting in mental weakness, or a troubled mind. Subjects may also experience great sadness at various times. They are emotional and can be very cruel, especially if they feel wronged by another. These are secretive, intense, jealous, seemingly unfeeling people who can prove dangerous if provoked and are not easy to understand, yet they are very sensitive.

They are sound business people, strong in purpose and can plot out their actions, seeing them through to the end. Often they have dark complexions and hair on the body. They may drink or take other types of intoxicants. Usually they are not close to their mother. Although these are intense people, they do have a spiritual nature and can be adept in meditation or mysticism.

MOON IN SAGITTARIUS

This is a sign ruled by Jupiter and instills a person with many positive qualities. They are honest, moral, generous, straightforward in their dealings with others and strive for great accomplishments. They are extremely intelligent and excellent communicators.

In business they may be successful and always try to be fair. They have sharp minds and are adept in the legal profession. They make intelligent use of their money and often spend it for the benefit of others. They are spiritualistic and philanthropic, faithful to their spouses and make ideal parents.

MOON IN CAPRICORN

Capricorn is ruled by the planet Saturn. It may give confidence in the occupation, leading to success. Subjects are good-hearted, but frequently change their minds about things. They love to help other people, but may also be less than kind at times. Generally patient people, who may be involved in yoga or meditation, they are steadfast and overcome problems. They have quick-witted minds and usually aspire to greatness, often as artists or writers. They have some humility to their credit. The body is often slender and the head large.

MOON IN AQUARIUS

Aquarius is under the rulership of Saturn and gives persons with the Moon here interest in philosophy and religion. There may also be interest in yoga, meditation and psychic perceptions. They are very discerning people, especially about the motives of others and can act as peacemakers. They don't usually have large appetites but may like to drink more than they should, especially as they enjoy the company of others. Often tall with a fair complexion, they are artistic and possess the energy to accomplish their work.

Moon in Aquarius may raise subjects up in life, then cause a severe drop in status. At some stages they may have a lot, materially, then at other times, seem to be poor. They can make powerful enemies but, when old, tend to withdraw into an unattached, spiritually motivated, consciousness.

MOON IN PISCES

This sign is under the rulership of Jupiter, so individuals with the Moon here will have knowledge of spiritual subject matters. They have sound discretion but often have difficulty making up their minds. Occasionally they can be too much affected by their emotions, which can possibly cloud their sensibilities or their judgement of matters. These are giving people who genuinely care for the trials and tribulations of others. Generally attractive people, with high intelligence, they are honest and easy-going, with amiable personalities. They make steadfast friends and can also be very romantic in their love lives.

MOON IN FIRST HOUSE

Good-looking, satisfied people, with a strong mind and may be psychic. They make reliable friendships and are extremely perceptive. Almost always they are involved in dealing with others in their career. They enjoy variety in their lives.

MOON IN SECOND HOUSE

These people are intelligent and learned. They are astute with finance and may be very successful at various times in their lives. They know how to treat others and are well-liked. They tend to have large families and a keen appetite. Inheritance is possible.

MOON IN THIRD HOUSE

These people may be somewhat unsettled within their minds and are not always straightforward. They like change and generally have trouble sticking to one job but would be suited as actors or narrators.
They are not the most generous people and may fight within their families.

MOON IN FOURTH HOUSE

These people are at peace with themselves and with others. They possess strong intelligence, foresight and make long-lasting friends. They usually own property in beautiful surroundings but tend to move frequently. They enjoy romance and the art of love.

MOON IN FIFTH HOUSE

These are trustworthy people that can go far in their careers and in life in general. They can be successful in obtaining properties and beautiful things. These people can have wonderful children and are capable of giving very worthwhile advice to others.

MOON IN SIXTH HOUSE

These people are spiritually inclined and have problems rising to positions of importance. They suffer from hostile people, loneliness at times, lack of a positive attitude and sickness as a youngster.

MOON IN SEVENTH HOUSE

These people are good-looking and very sexually inclined. They may exhibit jealousy, unfaithfulness and extreme emotions, making them subject to losing relationships. However, they can be helpful to others and often are successful in their careers.

MOON IN EIGHTH HOUSE

These people are generally attractive and well-built, although they may not be mentally stable all the time and want for companionship. They tend to have weak eyesight. Inheritance from the family is possible.

MOON IN NINTH HOUSE

This is a wonderful placement for the Moon, indicating a powerful mind and a philosophical attitude toward life.They may do a lot of travelling and are compassionate people. They are property owners and may attain success in their career. The mother is a wonderful person and they have pleasant children.

MOON IN TENTH HOUSE

These are creative and intelligent people who may be helpful to others. They usually live a long life and are philosophically inclined.

MOON IN ELEVENTH HOUSE

Good-looking and enjoyers of a fulfiling love life, these people have high intelligence and are skilled in making money but, can be very kind and helpful to others. Generally they like to keep their personal life private.

MOON IN TWELFTH HOUSE

This person may not have strong eyes and their mind may be troubled. They may be insular and inclined toward intoxication. They have many ups and downs in the career and, more often than not, don't have a good relationship with their mother. However, they are spiritually inclined.

MARS IN ARIES

Since Mars is the planet that rules this sign, it becomes very powerful. These are people with lots of energy and great forcefulness. They love to try new things and to visit different places. Property owners, they enjoy competition, sports and associating with other people, although they may be accident prone.

MARS IN TAURUS

These emotional people like to talk, but find it hard to accept opinions other than their own. They may be shy at times, but love to associate with the opposite sex.

MARS IN GEMINI

These attractive people may have high intelligence and be somewhat artistic but they are not the best of communicators. They may have sharp tongues which irritate and they are not known for their generosity or seeing things through to completion. All these points result in a lack of close friends or associates.

MARS IN CANCER
These people have considerable intelligence to their credit, but this is the weakest place for Mars and causes problems in marriage and relationships with other people. They may have agitated minds and disagree with others about their capabilities. They are not good at taking advice.

MARS IN LEO
These folks are basically strong, both physically and mentally and like the outdoors. They are goal-setters who like to see things through to completion. They are generous people who care for others, although there is often some contention in marriage, yet are often unsettled. They must take care of their health, especially the chest area.

MARS IN VIRGO
These people may be talented and be adept communicators but they also tend to be a little full of themselves, not really caring about others opinions of them. However, they may be fairly successful in their career. They are lusty and frequently do not have much discretion in regards to their love life.

MARS IN LIBRA
These people are usually good-looking and physically fit. They are successful in business and have sound discretion. They like the finer things in life. They may become angry when provoked and may have problems in marriage.

MARS IN SCORPIO
Mars is the ruler of this sign, making it strong. They have great energy to expend and may become quite successful. They are intelligent and said to be "sharp as a tack" mentally. They are successful in real estate and specialize in occupations not known to the general public.

MARS IN SAGITTARIUS
This sign is a beneficial place for Mars and gives success in many endeavours. Subjects are strong, energetic and helpful to society in general. They are extremely capable and may rise to high and respected positions in life. They tend to be very influential.

MARS IN CAPRICORN
This is the most powerful position for Mars. It is called "exalted" in this sign. Subjects are well educated, use their energy in many beneficial ways, not only for themselves but for others. They have many friends. Successful in their chosen career, often as doctors, soldiers, athletes or estate agents.

MARS IN AQUARIUS
These people are quite intelligent and have sound common sense, yet may act in ways they know are not for the best. They are powerful and many are fond of

them, but they may sometimes suffer from the envy of others. They keep things "bottled-up" inside, which makes them explode angrily on occasions. They may have a "mean streak" and an affinity for intoxication. Although they basically have kind hearts, they are rarely satisfied and are usually discontented.

MARS IN PISCES

These are friendly people, but indecisive and may also be moody. They are kind to others and usually have the greatest success in their career far from their place of birth.

MARS IN FIRST HOUSE

Subjects have great energy to achieve their aims in life and are of a strong physical constitution. Their love for competition makes them bicker and they may have problems in the marriage. They are usually property owners and work for things they believe in.

MARS IN SECOND HOUSE

Talkative and always ready to give their opinions, these gifted communicators may, naturally, work in the communication field. There may be instability in the birth family and they may be unfaithful to their spouse. They have large appetites and must take care of their teeth. More financial prosperity comes in the second half of their lives.

MARS IN THIRD HOUSE

Physically strong and determined mentally, they push themselves to achieve their goals in business and are talented in what they do. The possibility of losing a brother exists.

MARS IN FOURTH HOUSE

These people are quite intense, an aspect of their disposition which may become too much for their spouses, often causing break-up and divorce. They frequently become well-known in their sphere and usually are property owners.

MARS IN FIFTH HOUSE

Usually strong, influential and well educated they may excel as sportsmen, soldiers, or leaders. They are somewhat lacking in compassion and may have ups and downs in the career. They generally don't have many children and may have digestive problems.

MARS IN SIXTH HOUSE

Subjects tend to live away from their home towns and prefer the country over city life. They are good-looking and usually have a full love life. They tend to be a little overbearing and like to argue to make a point.

MARS IN SEVENTH HOUSE

These people have ample energy to accomplish any task and are excellent communicators, helping them to be successful in business and working with others. Their spouse will also be energetic and outspoken. They travel and may be property owners.

MARS IN EIGHTH HOUSE

These people may engage in illegal businesses or activities that get them into trouble with the law. They are strong people and may be good communicators as well, but have a tendency toward underhanded and dubious activities.

MARS IN NINTH HOUSE

Those so positioned may be philosophical and work hard for things they believe in. They need to control their anger and lower nature. As a result they often have legal problems and tend to spend on material goods, such as the home, cars, etc.

MARS IN TENTH HOUSE

These very strong, energetic and intense people are most capable in their work and duties in life. They throw themselves into whatever is required of them and may act hastily at times. They may be successful in the real estate business, automobile industry or anything involving machinery. They love competition and sports. Sometimes they are perceived as having a mean streak to their personality. Others may find fault with them and treat them badly.

MARS IN ELEVENTH HOUSE

Subjects have strength of character and the potency to accomplish what they set out to do. They often become prosperous and are influential over others but, outside of their work, may not have a large circle of friends or associates. They have small families and try to look at others as all part of a greater family.

MARS IN TWELFTH HOUSE

This placement is problematic for happiness at home or in work. Those so positioned may lose their husband or wife, due to being unfaithful and are not wise with their financial matters. They may be restless, always on the move and become easily dissatisfied. Sleepless nights are common, due to a restless mind. On the positive side they are helpful to others. They must take care of their teeth.

MERCURY IN ARIES

This is an intelligent and creative person with artistic talents, yet may be a little disorganized and devious. They like to read but are not generally interested in spiritual subject matters. They may be somewhat nervous.

MERCURY IN TAURUS

Friendly and artistic people, who will persevere until they succeed. They are usually attractive, well-mannered and popular, with a full love life.

MERCURY IN GEMINI

Mercury is the ruler of this sign and is strong in this position. Subjects are therefore excellent communicators with success in business, and more than one career. Many are artistic. They are intelligent and capable of doing many things at a fast pace. They may also get divorced and remarried.

MERCURY IN CANCER

Subjects are usually successful in the career but, despite a sense of humour, they are difficult to be close to due to a restless, argumentative and emotional nature.

MERCURY IN LEO

This person may be somewhat spiritually inclined but, usually, is lacking in discrimination and proper use of intelligence. They are very intent on sex and may be arrogant. They need to develop humility.

MERCURY IN VIRGO

This is the most powerful sign for Mercury and results in many positive attributes. Subjects are intelligent, well-educated and excellent communicators, allowing them success in business endeavours and all sorts of occupations dealing with other people. They are popular and they make sincere and helpful friends, whose advice is valuable. They are clean people with positive habits, religious and faithful to their spouses.

MERCURY IN LIBRA

These are people of upright character that care for others. They are interested in earning money and are careful with investments. They often take on different jobs and are most successful in communicative fields. They may overconsume, giving them health problems.

MERCURY IN SCORPIO

These people have problems in their relationships. They may be self-centred and treat people with disrespect. They have poor discretion and people do not feel comfortable with them. They should try to curb their tongue and develop humility.

MERCURY IN SAGITTARIUS

Those so influenced are intelligent, well educated and make outstanding teachers. They are straightforward, open-minded, have reliable friends and enjoy travelling.

MERCURY IN CAPRICORN

This is a business person who may not always be straightforward in his dealings. Money is a motivator but they may also get into debt. At times they associate with lower-class people and may be of a nervous nature. Physically they do not usually grow tall.

MERCURY IN AQUARIUS

These people are quite intelligent and scholarly. They usually enjoy a full education, are trustworthy and have very definitive opinions that are difficult to change. They may attain an advanced position.

MERCURY IN PISCES

This is the weakest sign for Mercury. Subjects may be restless, with poor discretion and misuse of intelligence. Marital relationships may be difficult and usually they have jobs requiring little intellectual input.

MERCURY IN FIRST HOUSE

This is an excellent placement for Mercury, giving many desirable qualities. Those so placed love variety in their lives and are fast and skillful in what they undertake. They are very intelligent and excellent communicators, making them successful in business or anything requiring dealing with other people.

MERCURY IN SECOND HOUSE

This is a beneficial placement allowing a measure of financial success and skillful use of money. Subjects like to talk and can speak before groups of people. They will probably be involved in writing or the communication field.

MERCURY IN THIRD HOUSE

These are talented people that can achieve success and complete what they set out to accomplish. They like to read and write. They may have wealthy friends or associates. Internally they may feel ill at ease and nervous but they manage to do what they must.

MERCURY IN FOURTH HOUSE

These people are very intelligent and know what they want in life. They are materially successful, owning their own homes and cars. They like natural surroundings and spending time with their families. They are kind, patient and can give sound advice to others.

MERCURY IN FIFTH HOUSE

These are intelligent, multi-talented people who are excellent communicators, making them outstanding teachers or able to give reliable advice to others. They are comfortable speaking before groups of people and may be called upon for their opinions in important matters. They may have large families and are also inclined toward spirituality.

MERCURY IN SIXTH HOUSE

This is an intelligent person, capable in their career and may achieve a leading position in business. They may be secretive or desiring to be alone as much as possible. They are interested in philosophy and overseas travel. They must beware of those hostile towards them.

MERCURY IN SEVENTH HOUSE

This is an intelligent and capable person who will have good successes and many friends. Such people communicate well and may be meticulous in their work. There is a possibility they will not stick to one career and may be travellers. Divorce and remarriage is not uncommon. They have spiritual motivations.

MERCURY IN EIGHTH HOUSE

This position gives high intelligence and an adequate education. Those so influenced have long life and interest in spiritual matters. They also may inherit money from their family. They may be somewhat fault-finding of others, which doesn't allow them a large circle of friends or well-wishers. They may also have weak nerves.

MERCURY IN NINTH HOUSE

Excellent placement, giving success in the career and many opportunities. They become known to others and are adept communicators. Career may involve commerce between cities or countries. They are religious, generous and helpful.

MERCURY IN TENTH HOUSE

These are great communicators, allowing success in many fields. They are well educated and earn through anything to do with sales or communication with other people.

MERCURY IN ELEVENTH HOUSE

This is a wonderful position. It makes for success, both materially and spiritually. Subjects have excellent friends, are intelligent and may become wealthy. Their influence may be wide spread.

MERCURY IN TWELFTH HOUSE

This placement is not beneficial for the career or financial stability. People in this position have difficulty in communication, thereby hampering material successes. However, they are kind-hearted people, who act in a proper manner and are spiritually inclined.

JUPITER IN ARIES
Good position giving fine qualities. Such people are trustworthy and helpful. They may have large families and the patience to instill respected standards and qualities in their children. Physically fit, with plenty of energy to accomplish their work, they like variety and travelling. They may be spiritually inclined.

JUPITER IN TAURUS
These people are somewhat stubborn and opinionated to the point of appearing arrogant at times, yet can be generous and kind. They are very attached to their spouse and the home environment, and like to enjoy the pleasures in life.

JUPITER IN GEMINI
These people may be excellent communicators with much learning and knowledge to their credit. Since they can make themselves easily understood, they make excellent teachers.

JUPITER IN CANCER
This is the most powerful position for Jupiter as it is exalted in Cancer. God has smiled upon these persons, indicating much piety in previous births. They tend to be wealthy, religious and blessed with excellent powers of perception. These charitable souls care for others and are just in their dealings.

JUPITER IN LEO
This is the Sun's sign and a beneficial placement for Jupiter. Those influenced may have myriad talents and excellent qualities, such as keen discretion and compassion for others. Religious and influential, they make outstanding leaders with an ability to communicate well.

JUPITER IN VIRGO
These people may have strong physical constitutions and earn a living through physical means. Subjects may be artistic or talented with their hands. An attractive marital partner may be gained, along with long-lasting friendships.

JUPITER IN LIBRA
Libra is ruled by Venus which results in these popular, attractive subjects having compassionate hearts and feeling for those around them. Although they enjoy comfortable living situations, marriage is often full of discontent and short-lived. They usually have a religious disposition and friends in fortunate positions.

JUPITER IN SCORPIO
These people may often seem extroverted to the point of conceit, yet can also be very intense in their dealings with others. Although they can work with great energy, they may earn money through illegal methods at times. They are inclined to have a revengeful nature, which they should try to overcome.

JUPITER IN SAGITTARIUS

Jupiter is the ruler of Sagittarius and positive qualities are usually manifest in families, homes, friends, and possessions. They possess high intelligence and are straightforward and honest. Much knowledge may be gained with Jupiter here, as well as financial prosperity.

JUPITER IN CAPRICORN

This is the weakest position and is termed the sign of debilitation for Jupiter. Those in this position may engage in illegalities for profit and may, at times, feel unfulfilled or cheated by life in general. Failures and trouble seem to follow them. Their families and/or relationships may be troublesome and unhappy.

JUPITER IN AQUARIUS

Those with this placement have an interest in philosophical subject matter and helping others. Unfortunately, they also have bad habits which result in poor health. They gain the assistance and trust of people close to them.

JUPITER IN PISCES

Jupiter is the ruler of Pisces with beneficial results, especially in respect to children and helping others. These are peacemakers with a generous attitude and sincerity in their words and actions. Considerable financial gains should also manifest during the life.

JUPITER IN FIRST HOUSE

These persons are attractive, have a striking countenance and enjoy robust physical health. They are fair and just in their treatment of others and make fine teachers or leaders. They are religious and studied in philosophy. They usually experience long, fulfiling lives.

JUPITER IN SECOND HOUSE

These people are family oriented. They may also be learned and make a living through their intellectual capabilities, whether it be material or spiritual knowledge. They tend to have helpful partners and love to talk with other people on a variety of topics.

JUPITER IN THIRD HOUSE

Although they are quite intellectual, subjects may, at times, be thought of as insensitive and mean. They have powerful friends and are adept in communication. They get help from within their families and have good marriage partners.

JUPITER IN FOURTH HOUSE

These people have congenial friends and families. They give and receive profound advice. They may be conscientious and moralistic in their activities. As the fourth house indicates real estate, Jupiter here may give ownership of valuable land and/or property.

JUPITER IN FIFTH HOUSE

These affable people are appreciated by friends and family, being givers of sound advice or instruction. They are successful in making their holdings increase and may become well-known.

JUPITER IN SIXTH HOUSE

Those influenced usually enjoy strong physical health but mentally, may be egotistical, fighting with others. They spend their money easily on impermanent things. Often they assist a highly placed person in business or politics. They have few children and are travellers.

JUPITER IN SEVENTH HOUSE

This house represents the spouse, partners or friends and Jupiter here gives pleasing results in these matters. They are kind, giving people and are adept at financial arrangements. These subjects earn a living through partners, within or outside of the marriage.

JUPITER IN EIGHTH HOUSE

These people may have internal physical problems, although frequently they live to a ripe old age. They may be somewhat deceitful and have problems in marriage. Rarely are they in leadership positions.

JUPITER IN NINTH HOUSE

The ninth house, being the "house of good fortune", Jupiter here makes for religious and law-abiding people, often becoming respected leaders. Usually they are financially secure. Wisdom is gained, often through travel.

JUPITER IN TENTH HOUSE

Subjects may be a part of "high society", gaining the confidence of wealthy and influential people. Their occupation may be beneficial to many others and they may be involved with teaching, preaching a message or with finance.

JUPITER IN ELEVENTH HOUSE

Such people are good money-managers, being thrifty rather than exorbitant. Profit and gain are attained with little endeavour. They are brave and usually very influential people, living happily to an old age.

JUPITER IN TWELFTH HOUSE

These people tend to be unhappy with their positions in society and may desire to withdraw from the hustle-bustle. Whilst they are discontent with their quota in life, when older, they perform works leading to a positive future. However, family life may weigh down on them.

VENUS IN ARIES
These extroverts like to have fun in life but they do have some undesirable traits that may be embarrassing to others, unless they learn to control their lower nature. They marry a reliable partner but, at times they disagree.

VENUS IN TAURUS
These are good-looking persons with a healthy physical constitution. They are kind and have compassion for those less fortunate. They are very sensual and desire material things, yet have religious and philosophical yearnings within their hearts. They usually have a full love life and marry someone quite attractive.

VENUS IN GEMINI
These are people that are intelligent, educated and very sexually inclined. They have success in obtaining material things but also have a philosophical side. They are prone to be artistic, musically inclined and have amiable and agreeable associates.

VENUS IN CANCER
These people are attractive and congenial. They may be somewhat shy but they are very sensual, although they sometimes have upsets in their love life. They can be successful entertainers or earn a living through artistic enterprise. They usually have adequate finance in their lives.

VENUS IN LEO
These are people that like art, beauty and being in "high society" They are sensual people, proud of their accomplishments and usually marry an attractive spouse. However, they don't generally have large families.

VENUS IN VIRGO
Those so influenced tend to be learned and philosophically inclined but have problems with the material side of life. They are inclined to have losses of things they own, be put into financial difficulty or do unworthy things to make money. They may have problems in marriage and are subject to health problems, especially with the genitals or elimination system of the body.

VENUS IN LIBRA
These are beautiful people that get many pleasures in life. They are very sensual and have an active love life. They gain much opulence such as homes, jewels and the things that money can buy. They are successful and have trustworthy friends in powerful stations in life.

VENUS IN SCORPIO
Subjects have a powerful physical constitution and are usually very sexually inclined. Indeed they often have a tumultuous love life, and need to learn to control their lower nature. They like to live in beautiful environments and enjoy art and

music. They are often psychic or have spiritual leanings, but can be mean and vengeful at times. They are argumentative and may, consequently, suffer legal problems.

VENUS IN SAGITTARIUS

These people are inclined towards both spirituality and materialism, experiencing a push-pull effect between the two sides. They are good-looking, educated, have reliable friends and live in comfort. Others like and respect them.

VENUS IN CAPRICORN

This is a good-looking person but may not have a strong physical constitution and may be subject to heart problems. Subjects are not overly moralistic and may do things, for profit, that are not in their best interests. Usually they marry someone older than they are that they must depend on to take care of them. They have pleasant friends and like to travel.

VENUS IN AQUARIUS

This is an affable, positive person with an unobtrusive personality. Such people love to have fun, go to parties and be with others. These people are also sensually inclined and should watch their lower desires from becoming too strong.

VENUS IN PISCES

This is the most powerful sign for Venus. It indicates an intelligent, educated person that has spiritual leanings and the ability to gain anything they may desire. Subjects will have good friends, lovers, homes, etc. They can also be a very beneficial influence on others.

VENUS IN FIRST HOUSE

These are beautiful people that experience many of the pleasurable, sensual things in life. They are charitable, speak well and can teach others. They may also be artists, musicians or dancers. They generally have a well appointed home, expensive automobiles and a great love life. They must be careful of sickness coming from overconsumption of the so called "good things in life".

VENUS IN SECOND HOUSE

This is a good-looking person that is an adept communicator, with a tendency to be artistic and has no lacking in finances. Such people frequently possess valuable properties and all sorts of beautiful things, such as valuable gemstones,etc. They are quite sensual and are generally very successful and satisfied.

VENUS IN THIRD HOUSE

This is a smart, capable person that is an excellent communicator, possibly as an author or in business affairs. Those in this position aren't usually wealthy but have satisfactory success in their careers and an enjoyable family life.

VENUS IN FOURTH HOUSE

This is a wonderful person that is compassionate and is someone to look up to. They are intelligent, educated and achieve great success in life. Such people get to live in well furnished homes in pleasant environments, have expensive cars and possessions, enjoy family life and friends and have satisfying love lives.

VENUS IN FIFTH HOUSE

This person is intelligent, educated and capable of giving excellent advice. Such people tend to be successful, both materially and spiritually. They may become rich and have affable families. They often have connection to, or involvement with, the entertainment field.

VENUS IN SIXTH HOUSE

These are trustworthy, reliable, popular and respected people. They like to travel and get ample opportunity. They have to spend a lot on the upkeep of their home and vehicles. They usually don't have large families.

VENUS IN SEVENTH HOUSE

These subjects are intelligent, educated and attractive people that have amiable friends and get along well with others. They are successful business people and have lots of energy. They could have problems in marriage or sometimes they take a long time to find someone they wish to marry. They may be very sexually inclined or sometimes they decide to completely abstain from a physical love life. These are travellers.

VENUS IN EIGHTH HOUSE

This is generally a spiritually inclined person that lives a long life. They may marry later in life, or sometimes experience divorce and remarriage. They may possess land and/or property.

VENUS IN NINTH HOUSE

These are intelligent people that are materially successful, as well as possessing a religious and philosophical mind. They are generous, artistic and have many valuable possessions. They have a beautiful spouse and pleasant families. There is much opportunity for travel.

VENUS IN TENTH HOUSE

These are intelligent people with good education and many capabilities. They may be artists, writers, musicians, or athletes or do well in occupations such as a beautician, the medical field or the world of entertainers. These people are likeable and gain many important friends. They usually have expensive homes, vehicles and possessions, and tend to hold sway over others.

VENUS IN ELEVENTH HOUSE

These are intelligent and influential people that are very successful in life.

They are affable people that get a good spouse, children and have more than adequate finances, without working too hard.

VENUS IN TWELFTH HOUSE

These are philosophical people that care for others but are too sensual for their own good. They are inclined to overindulge in the so-called "pleasurable things of life" to the detriment of their spiritual progress. They need to be more open and honest with themselves, as well as others.

SATURN IN ARIES

This is the weakest sign for Saturn and tends to cause subjects to act in unintelligent ways, giving a lack of close friends and causes marital problems. They may have a mean streak and be envious of others. They can engage in illegalities and experience a lack of success in their career. Back problems or weak teeth are not uncommon.

SATURN IN TAURUS

This is a favourable sign for Saturn. These are honest and reliable working people. They will be intelligent about their expenditures of money. They enjoy food and have large appetites. These folks like their privacy and may have several marriages.

SATURN IN GEMINI

This is a another beneficial place for Saturn and endows people with intelligence and a capability for success. Subjects may have two sides to them, one being pleasant, honest and helpful and the other, unfortunately, being just the opposite. They usually enjoy spending time in the open air.

SATURN IN CANCER

This is not a great place for Saturn and may result in a restless mind. Subjects may also move around a lot and have a negative outlook on life. As children they may have health problems and their relationship with their own children may not be the best. There may be weakness in the teeth.

SATURN IN LEO

This is another weak sign for Saturn and may make those involved a little difficult to get along with. They are capable and can be responsible but have a hard time taking direction from others. They may be somewhat spiritually inclined. There may be problems in marriage and physically with the heart and digestion.

SATURN IN VIRGO

This is a good sign for Saturn and often makes for success in the career. It gives excellent communicative abilities and the ability to lead. These attractive people are careful, yet may be argumentative at times.

SATURN IN LIBRA

This is the most powerful sign for Saturn to be situated in. It can give a long life, strong influence and great success in the career. Those concerned may become wealthy and also have potential in yoga, meditation and/or mysticism.

SATURN IN SCORPIO

These people live interesting, action-packed lives but there may be many negative implications from this placement. It may make subjects get into lowly jobs or illegalities that can result in legal ramifications. They may act without thinking and have losses in the career.

SATURN IN SAGITTARIUS

This is a fortuitous placement. Those so influenced should have interest in spirituality, high intelligence, honesty and be generous. They have a correct attitude about life and other people, are faithful in marriage and usually have pleasant children. These are knowledgeable and just people.

SATURN IN CAPRICORN

Saturn is also the ruler of this sign and is quite strong here. Often subjects live far from their place of birth. They make advancement through marriage and may do business with things which come from the earth. They have strong will power and concern for those less fortunate. They may be artistic and subject to moodiness.

SATURN IN AQUARIUS

Saturn is the ruler of Aquarius and so is well situated here. Those affected are sound, ingenious people, interested in philosophical things and spirituality. They are likable, but are often somewhat eccentric. They enjoy drinking and are sexually inclined.

SATURN IN PISCES

This is a positive sign for Saturn. There may be great success in the career and a harmonious relationship with the spouse and family. Subjects will be moralistic, trustworthy and shrewd money managers. They will have many friends that appreciate them. Later in life they tend to become reclusive and yearn for spiritual knowledge.

SATURN IN FIRST HOUSE

These are correct, honest persons who are "slow but sure" and help others. They like to travel and are comfortable wherever they are. They experience myriad problems when young and are prone to also have difficulties in the marriage relationship.

SATURN IN SECOND HOUSE

These people have a lot of ups and downs and have family problems. They are hard workers and like to do large business deals, in which they often are successful.

SATURN IN THIRD HOUSE

These are strong people who are skilled workers and relate well with partners. However, their mental condition sometimes is hostile to others and they may have family troubles, or suffer loss of children.

SATURN IN FOURTH HOUSE

These are travellers that often are found working away from their home or place of birth. They are pleasant people that do not require much to be satisfied. They may have health problems in the chest area.

SATURN IN FIFTH HOUSE

These people are conscientious and capable of teaching others or giving correct advice. They are not very romantic and, indeed, are frequently unhappy with their love lives. They may have stomach or digestive problems.

SATURN IN SIXTH HOUSE

These are strong people, capable of overcoming problems or those that come up against them. They frequently work in more than one field and often find success in real estate. They sometimes appear to be somewhat arrogant.

SATURN IN SEVENTH HOUSE

These people are travellers and may even get married to a foreigner. They tend to work in more than one occupation and be involved in illegal businesses for profit. They appear unemotional or unconcerned with others. Physically they may have hearing problems.

SATURN IN EIGHTH HOUSE

These people are capable in their careers but may be dishonest, unfaithful and unsocial. There could be separation from their children. There may be poor eyesight and problems with the body's elimination system.

SATURN IN NINTH HOUSE

These people are interested in philosophical and spiritual subject matters. They are prone to have problems with their superiors. They should become interested in politics or helping the poor. Physically, they are likely to have digestive problems.

SATURN IN TENTH HOUSE

These are generally honest, righteous people but may get involved in things or with people that get them into trouble. They have goals and work steadfastly to achieve them. They tend to have more than one marriage since the spouse may die before they do. They are successful in business with things that come from the earth. They travel to foreign lands and have severe ups and downs in life.

SATURN IN ELEVENTH HOUSE

These are strong, hard working people who may become influential. They usually live and work far from the birthplace. They are successful in business with things that come from mother earth.

SATURN IN TWELFTH HOUSE

These are hard workers that, unfortunately, will have many problems. They suffer losses and have times in life when they are confined or forced to stay in an undesirable place. They are inclined to be secretive people, not liking to be bothered.

In this following section remember that Rahu and Ketu act like Saturn and Mars respectively and will also pick up the traits of the ruler of the sign in which they are situated. To understand how Rahu or Ketu will act in a particular sign, look to how Saturn or Mars would be in that sign, how they are actually situated and also to the ruler of the sign in which it is situated (if Virgo, look to Mercury; if Pisces, look to Jupiter, etc.) to see that planet's strength, or weakness. The following is a list of general descriptions of Rahu and Ketu in the houses.

RAHU IN FIRST HOUSE

These people may be somewhat unusual. They are very sexually inclined and experience divorce and remarriage. They tend to also be interested in spiritual subject matters.

RAHU IN SECOND HOUSE

These people are well intentioned but tend to be too talkative. Furthermore, they are not faithful to their mates and may also be attracted to smoking and intoxication. They suffer fluctuations in their career and financial situation, leading to debts. They may do illegal businesses, at times, for profit.

RAHU IN THIRD HOUSE

This position may cause problems both with brothers and within the marital relationship. People so governed may be successful in the career but are very opinionated, which bothers others at times. However, they can be stoic and patient.

RAHU IN FOURTH HOUSE

These people generally live far from their place of birth. They may be influential but also sometimes believe in others when they shouldn't. They often have associates that are not a beneficial influence for their own progress in life.

RAHU IN FIFTH HOUSE

These persons like entertainment and games but are not satisfied within their minds. They won't have large families and may suffer the loss of a child or children. These subjects don't always use their intellect, consequently they suffer and they have rocky love lives and emotional upheavals.

RAHU IN SIXTH HOUSE

These are hard working people who often prevail over others. They may have long lives and like to travel overseas. They are likely, physically, to suffer problems with the elimination system of the body.

RAHU IN SEVENTH HOUSE

These people keep much inside themselves. They may be powerful and communicate well, although their minds may be troubled. Marriage could be difficult in general and, in particular, their spouse may be unfaithful to them.

RAHU IN EIGHTH HOUSE

These people have some redeeming qualities to their credit but they may be disagreeable and earn a living by illegal means. Others are, usually, not happy with their actions.

RAHU IN NINTH HOUSE

These are definitely philosophical but also intense persons. They are politically far to the left and may be involved in criminal actions. At times they may have some power over others, but it is not long lasting.

RAHU IN TENTH HOUSE

This is a good position for Rahu and helps subjects to become successful in their career. They may become wealthy and achieve a high position in life. They work for the benefit of others and usually are philosophically and/or artistically inclined.

RAHU IN ELEVENTH HOUSE

This placement is the optimum, giving powerful, successful people that are self-controlled and should have great influence. They are helpful to spiritualists. On the down side they may have a deficiency in their hearing and may, at times, experience set backs of a general nature.

RAHU IN TWELFTH HOUSE

These people may suffer from disturbed sleep and poor eyesight. Digestive problems are also not uncommon. They will probably travel or move around a lot and may be dissatisfied with their love life.

KETU IN FIRST HOUSE

Those in this position are likely to be interested in the occult and/or spirituality. They are often mental dreamers with visions. Physically they may have an emaciated or skinny appearance. Not a strong placement for a long lifetime or material happiness.

KETU IN SECOND HOUSE

This is not a good position for financial or familial stability. Those so governed must also learn to take care in what they eat. Speech problems and poor eyesight are indicated here also.

KETU IN THIRD HOUSE

This indicates strength of mind, giving the power to prevail over others in competition. Close family bonds, although, unfortunately, subjects may experience loss of a brother. May have physical debility in a limb.

KETU IN FOURTH HOUSE

This position gives spiritual interests but, materially, many losses of possessions. Not ideal for either the maternal relationship or for long-lasting friendships. Indicates fluctuations in career and a residence far from place of birth.

KETU IN FIFTH HOUSE

Despite high intellect, much mental distress is indicated, together with losses of finance, a small family and few friends. Subjects are susceptible to allergic reactions and digestive weakness.

KETU IN SIXTH HOUSE

This is a beneficial placement for Ketu and those so governed are likely to be powerful and find enjoyments in life. They tend to have common sense and generally are able to fulfil their desires. May be the most successful or powerful person in the birth family. Problems could be had with vision and the teeth.

KETU IN SEVENTH HOUSE

Subjects should guard against thieves and physically may have digestive or intestinal problems. May be famous but reclusive, with a marriage partner considered strange by others.

KETU IN EIGHTH HOUSE

Beware of enemies! Not an ideal placement for success in career or for long life. Bowel problems may arise on the physical side. Many material losses are indicated. Subjects engage in harmful activities for profit. However, often they have mystical or psychic abilities.

KETU IN NINTH HOUSE

Indicates a courageous person who cares for the upliftment of others. This is not good for business success or pleasing superiors. Subjects are prone to anger easily and family problems do not help this. There are also difficulties while travelling.

KETU IN TENTH HOUSE

This position makes for hard work, with slow end results, but which may be helpful to the population at large. Subjects are well-liked, but not by all. Travel is indicated especially to temples, churches, or mosques.

KETU IN ELEVENTH HOUSE
Indicates influential, charitably minded people, with spiritual connotations, who realize their goals in life. However, they could be distressed, due to poor choice of associates and, physically, from digestive problems.

KETU IN TWELFTH HOUSE
Indicates myriad problems and/or losses of money and energy. Subjects have difficulty sleeping peacefully and obtain little pleasure from their love life. They may be spiritually inclined, but the material life is fraught with insecurity. Subjects are physically prone to weak eyes.

THE STARS

In addition to the twelve signs of the zodiac there are twenty-seven stars, also known as "Nakshatras", that are extremely important in astrology. Each star covers an area of 13 degrees 20 minutes so some overlap different signs. They will give more precise information of specific traits besides those indicated by the zodiacal sign and are the basis for choosing correct days and times to begin specific activities. Timing is very important to the results of an endeavour, therefore one branch of astrology is concerned with finding an auspicious time to begin things, which will, in turn, bring more chance of a successful result.

In a birth chart the influences of the stars are also extremely important, especially in reference to the rising star and Moon star. Each nakshatra covers a specific area within one or two signs. The following text will delineate the exact degrees within the signs where the nakshatras begin and end and the specific traits which result.

ASHWINI
(0 degrees through 13-20 degrees Aries)

RISING STAR IS ASHWINI
These are well-dressed, good-looking people that have many friends. They have strong morals, are quite capable in the career, determined and have a positive outlook on life. They have some humility, and find success.

MOONSTAR IS ASHWINI
These attractive people are intelligent, discreet, pleasant and of a satisfied nature. They can be inspirational to others. They love to travel.

BHARANI
(13-20 degrees through 26-40 degrees Aries)

RISING STAR IS BHARANI
These are brave, helpful people, who, while very sexually inclined, usually have small families. They can be gullible and may suffer from the envy of others. They generally have a good life span.

MOON STAR IS BHARANI
These people are physically healthy, talented in their career, and satisfied with their accomplishments.

KARTTIKA
(26-40 degrees Aries through 10 degrees Taurus)

RISING STAR IS KARTTIKA
These are very capable, heroic type persons that like to be in control and have high aspirations. They are honest, have good manners, and are usually successful, materially.

MOON STAR IS KARTTIKA

These people may be determined to do what they set out to do, but often waiver mentally. They like to eat a lot, may be handsome in appearance and possibly famous in their circles.

ROHINI
(10 degrees through 23-20 degrees Taurus)

RISING STAR IS ROHINI

These are good-looking, popular, capable people that may be found in leadership positions. They are philosophical, yet at times tend to be critical of others. They have a satisfying love life and generally are successful in their careers. They may go away from their parents when young and physically may have poor eyesight.

MOON STAR IS ROHINI

These people tend to be beautiful and be blessed with a wonderful nature. They are honest, self disciplined and nonenvious.

MIRGASHIRA
(23-20 degrees Taurus through 6-40 degrees Gemini)

RISING STAR IS MIRGASHIRA

These are beautiful people that like the finer things of life. They are fairly energetic, intelligent and like to learn a variety of things. They like to talk and sing. They are close to their mothers, but may have health problems in their youth.

MOON STAR IS MIRGASHIRA

Subjects may be affluent, gaining many pleasures in life. They are sensual, yet sometimes shy. Intelligent and hard workers, they avoid controversy and conflict, whenever possible.

ARDRA
(6-40 degrees through 20 degrees Gemini)

RISING STAR IS ARDRA

These people usually end up in an intellectually unstimulating position. They are physically strong and usually live a long life but may have tendencies to want to take what is not their own at times. They may also be critical of others.

MOON STAR IS ARDRA

This indicates people with a mean streak that may cause pain to others, or, conversely, it may indicate compassion for others in pain. Subjects may be somewhat arrogant and/or play tricks on others at times.

PUNARVASU
(20 degrees Gemini through 3-20 degrees Cancer)

RISING STAR IS PUNARVASU

These are generous, intelligent and contented people who enjoy life. They like to move around and have a hard time committing to a relationship. Often they have self doubts and suffer from indecision.

MOON STAR IS PUNARVASU

These people have amiable personalities and seem to be fairly self-controlled and contented. Physically they may be bothered by sickness.

PUSHYA
(3-20 degrees through 16-40 degrees Cancer)

RISING STAR IS PUSHYA

These are wonderfully considerate, thoughtful, sincere and philosophical people. Good communicators, they generally become quite successful in their career. They are responsible family members.

MOON STAR IS PUSHYA

These popular people are very intelligent, with much knowledge. They are fairly pious and have controlled minds.

ASHLESHA
(16-40 degrees Cancer through 0 degrees Leo)

RISING STAR IS ASHLESHA

These people have much energy but need to learn how to channel it into more noble pursuits. They may be a little unkind to others and are uncomfortable in groups of people outside of their immediate friendship circle.

MOON STAR IS ASHLESHA

These people may have trouble regulating their eating habits. They may be strong but are prone to bad habits.

MAGHA
(0 degrees through 13-20 degrees Leo)

RISING STAR IS MAGHA

These are very intelligent, well mannered and extremely successful people. They may become rich and gain much happiness in life. People like them but they, themselves, have a distaste for particular persons that they, at times come into contact with. They are achievers and get their jobs done as needed. They are sensually inclined but also have a religious nature.

MOON STAR IS MAGHA

These people may be affluent and obtain many pleasures in life. They may be attractive and powerful physically. They are honest, charitable and successful people.

PURVAPHALGUNI
(13-20 degrees through 26-40 degrees Leo)

RISING STAR IS PURVAPHALGUNI

These are very energetic people with a healthy physical constitution. They are well suited to positions of authority for they are kind and generous. They like action in their lives.

MOON STAR IS PURVAPHALGUNI

These people have a shining countenance and are very open minded as to what other people may do. They are faithful to what, or whom, they may believe in and like to travel.

UTTARAPHALGUNI
(26-40 degrees Leo through 10 degrees Virgo)

RISING STAR IS UTTARAPHALGUNI

These are good-looking and intelligent people that become successful in the career. They may become wealthy and have a high opinion of themselves. They are very sensually inclined and have a varied love life.

MOON STAR IS UTTARAPHALGUNI

These attractive, popular people may be teachers, leaders or involved in research. They are contented and kind. Materially they are inclined to purchase property.

HASTA
(10 degrees through 23-20 degrees Virgo)

RISING STAR IS HASTA

These are capable people with an attractive disposition, good at communicating and enjoy travelling. They are determined and somewhat conservative in their actions. They care for and like to socialize with others.

MOON STAR IS HASTA

These people need to control their lower nature. They are conscientious workers but like to drink or take other intoxicants and may, as a result, become obnoxious.

CHITRA
(23-20 degrees Virgo through 6-40 degrees Libra)

RISING STAR IS CHITRA
These people usually move far from the home town. They like beautiful clothes and jewellry and have a strong and active love life. Often they have many different interests. At times they can be a little condescending towards others.

MOON STAR IS CHITRA
This indicates a person that has alluring eyes and a gorgeous body.

SWATI
(6-40 degrees through 20 degrees Libra)

RISING STAR IS SWATI
These are kind and seemingly self-satisfied people who take their time in doing things, so much so that others may think they're not very capable. They do not live in the place they were born and have religious inclinations.

MOON STAR IS SWATI
These people are honest and have a pleasant disposition. They have some humility and care about others. They speak well and are very capable in business.

VISHAKHA
(20 degrees Libra through 3-20 degrees Scorpio)

RISING STAR IS VISHAKHA
These may be philosophical people that have knowledge. They are energetic, like to talk but have little patience and can quickly become upset. They should try to gain more self-control. They may become wealthy.

MOON STAR IS VISHAKHA
These people are excellent communicators and have a pleasant aura about them. Unfortunately they also have an argumentative and jealous side, which can result in disagreements.

ANURADHA
(3-20 degrees through 16-40 degrees Scorpio)

RISING STAR IS ANURADHA
These attractive people are generally 'spiritualists', although they may become somewhat depressed at times. They are rather shy in groups of people but love being with their families. They usually live away from the town in which they were born and enjoy travel.

MOON STAR IS ANURADHA

Attractive people who are kind and especially like to be with their families. They may be somewhat shy around groups of people. They also enjoy travelling.

JYESTHA

(16-40 degrees Scorpio through 0 degrees Sagittarius)

RISING STAR IS JYESTHA

These are respectable people that are extremely capable of accomplishing their goals in life. Others may look up to them and they may have fair sized families or a good number of associates. They act and speak well and are very sensually inclined.

MOON STAR IS JYESTHA

Subjects may be generally satisfied, happy and have worthwhile qualities but they may, at times, be moody.

MULA

(0 degrees through 13-20 degrees Sagittarius)

RISING STAR IS MULA

These are intelligent and good-looking people that may be troubled by sickness at various times. They are knowledgeable and are goal setters, although the mind occasionally may be a little wavering. They have problems within the marriage.

MOON STAR IS MULA

These affable, but determined people, are fairly successful in life. They are satisfied with their accomplishments and like to live well.

PURVASHADHA

(13-20 degrees through 26-40 degrees Sagittarius)

RISING STAR IS PURVASHADHA

Subjects may not have a very advanced education but often have humility, making them pleasant to be around. They are very social people and often have large families and/or circle of friends.

MOON STAR IS PURVASHADHA

These people make excellent friends and are fair to all. They are faithful and happy in life. They also usually have a spouse with many good qualities.

UTTARASHADHA
(26-40 degrees Sagittarius through 10 degrees Capricorn)

RISING STAR IS UTTARASHADHA
Intelligent, fun-loving people, who may become well known. They are sensually inclined and have a varied love life. They must beware of enemies. They are generous and kind towards others and are wise counsellors.

MOON STAR IS UTTARASHADHA
These friendly people have good manners and many other fine qualities. They are appreciative of others and usually have a wide circle of friends.

SHRAVAN
(10 degrees through 23-20 degrees Capricorn)

RISING STAR IS SHRAVAN
These are intelligent people that have a sound education. They generally move away from where they were born, are philosophically inclined and have small families. They may become famous but they must beware of enemies.

MOON STAR IS SHRAVAN
These people are quick learners and usually gain much knowledge. They may become rich and well-known. Usually they also have a kind and well disposed spouse.

DHANISHTA
(23-20 degrees Capricorn through 6-40 degrees Aquarius)

RISING STAR IS DHANISHTHA
These are usually strong people that may be generous at various times. They have strong egos and may engage in "confrontation" within the marriage.

MOON STAR IS DHANISHTHA
This person lusts after acquisition and may become rich, yet is also generous. They may be brave and a little reckless. They like to listen to music.

SATABISHA
(6-40 degrees through 20 degrees Aquarius)

RISING STAR IS SATABISHA
These are philosophical, unobtrusive people that usually don't have many children. They usually assist others in their work. They can have a devious aspect to their nature.

MOON STAR IS SATABISHA

These people have problems in life but are brave and usually prevail over those that come up against them. They may be a bit stubborn, due to their experiences.

PURVABHADRAPADA
(20 degrees Aquarius through 3-20 degrees Pisces)

RISING STAR IS PURVABHADRAPADA

These are hard-working people that like to frequently relocate. They may have unusual methods of accomplishing their objectives. They are philosophical people, but extremely sensually inclined as well. They may be somewhat nervous in nature but live long lives.

MOON STAR IS PURVABHADRAPADA

These people may be constantly harassed by their spouse or family. They are extremely capable in their career and may become rich but are not known for their generosity.

UTTARABHADRAPADA
(3-20 degrees through 16-40 degrees Pisces)

RISING STAR IS UTTARABHADRAPADA

These people are a little eccentric. They are a bit shy but can speak well. They have a desire to become rich and change their minds a lot. They are somewhat philosophical, love their families but must be careful of enemies.

MOON STAR IS UTTARABHADRAPADA

These people are satisfied in life and are good communicators. They have many outstanding qualities and are helpful to others. They love their families and prevail over those that may be opposed to them.

REVATI
(16-40 degrees Pisces through 0 degrees Aries)

RISING STAR IS REVATI

These are good-looking, well mannered and brave people that may be very successful in their endeavours. They have a good physical constitution and nice habits. They are sensual, get along well with others and are adept at giving intelligent advice.

MOON STAR IS REVATI

These people are popular, pleasant looking, have good hygienic habits and mental fortitude.

TEMPORARY NATURE OF PLANETS

As stated earlier, the planets have benefic or malefic (positive and negative) natures. Jupiter, Venus, Moon, and Mercury are natural benefics and Sun, Mars, Saturn, Rahu, and Ketu are natural malefics. Rahu and Ketu are almost always malefic, except in rare circumstances, but the other planets have a "temporary" nature as malefic or benefic, according to the rising sign. Therefore, when interpreting the horoscope and/or making predictions, the natural qualities, as well as the temporary nature of a planet, must be taken into account.

The following are the temporary natures of the planets, according to the rising sign. The reasoning behind this is that certain houses are considered auspicious and certain others are considered inauspicious, according to the categories of life that the houses rule over. Sometimes naturally benefic planets rule malefic houses (due to sign ownership) and naturally malefic planets rule benefic houses. For example, under Taurus rising Jupiter and the Moon are temporary malefics as Jupiter owns the eighth and eleventh houses, and the Moon rules the third house, none of which are considered to be auspicious houses.

Furthermore, according to the rising sign, a planet may be considered neutral and one planet may be considered a "yoga-karaka", or the most powerful planet in the chart.

For the following rising signs, or ascendants (meaning this sign is in the first house of the horoscope), the planets take on temporary natures, as follows:

ARIES RISING

Jupiter, Mars and Sun are benefic rulers. Venus, Saturn, and Mercury are malefic rulers. Moon is neutral.

TAURUS RISING

Mercury, Sun and Venus are benefic rulers. Moon and Jupiter are malefic rulers. Mars is neutral. Saturn is yoga-karaka.

GEMINI RISING

Saturn, Mercury, and Venus are benefic rulers. Jupiter, Mars and Sun are malefic rulers. Moon is neutral.

CANCER RISING

Jupiter and Moon are benefic rulers. Venus, Mercury and Saturn are malefic rulers. Sun is neutral. Mars is yoga-karaka.

LEO RISING

Jupiter and Sun are benefic rulers. Saturn, Mercury and Venus are malefic rulers. Moon is neutral. Mars is yoga-karaka.

VIRGO RISING
Mercury and Venus are benefic rulers. Jupiter, Mars and Moon are malefic rulers. Saturn and Sun are neutral.

LIBRA RISING
Venus, Moon and Mercury are benefic rulers. Jupiter, Sun and Mars are malefic rulers. Saturn is yoga-karaka.

SCORPIO RISING
Jupiter, Sun, Moon and Mars are benefic rulers. Saturn, Mercury and Venus are malefic rulers.

SAGITTARIUS RISING
Jupiter, Mars and Sun are benefic rulers. Mercury, Saturn and Venus are malefic rulers. Moon is neutral.

CAPRICORN RISING
Mercury and Saturn are benefic rulers. Mars, Jupiter and Moon are malefic rulers. Sun is neutral. Venus is yoga-karaka.

AQUARIUS RISING
Mars, Sun, Mercury and Saturn are benefic rulers. Moon and Jupiter are malefic rulers. Venus is yoga-karaka.

PISCES RISING
Jupiter, Moon and Mars are benefic rulers. Venus, Saturn, Sun and Mercury are malefic rulers.

RULERSHIP (LORDSHIP) YOGAS

Another important tool for interpreting the horoscope is the rulership or lordship yogas. We have already delineated the rulers or lords of the particular signs, i.e., Sun is ruler (lord) of Leo; Moon is ruler of Cancer; Mars is ruler of Aries and Scorpio; Mercury is ruler of Gemini and Virgo; Jupiter is ruler of Sagittarius and Pisces; Venus is ruler of Taurus and Libra; Saturn is ruler of Capricorn and Aquarius.

Therefore, according to which sign is rising in the horoscope, the planets will own different houses, as the signs they own will also be in different houses. For example, for Aries rising, Mars owns the first house and the eighth house as Mars rules Aries and Scorpio. As another example: for Gemini rising, Mars rules the sixth and eleventh houses as Scorpio and Aries occupy these houses respectively. Again, if Aries is rising in the horoscope and Mars is occupying the third house, then we would say that Mars is the ruler, or lord, of the first house in the third house. It would also be ruler of the eighth house in the third house.

The following are a list of rulership yogas, by houses and the traits which are associated with those individuals so influenced.

RULER OF THE FIRST HOUSE

RULER OF FIRST HOUSE IN FIRST

Subjects are well built physically and good-looking. They are independent and may be seen as conceited by others. They may become famous and usually have more than one mate.

RULER OF FIRST HOUSE IN SECOND

Subjects are kind, generous people, with good discretion. Loves family life, but has small family. A sound business person who make a success of ventures.

RULER OF FIRST HOUSE IN THIRD

These people usually have more than one marriage. They are outspoken, with myriad talents. They tend to be kind and are admired.

RULER OF FIRST HOUSE IN FOURTH

Subjects are successful in gaining possessions, such as homes and cars. They are popular due to their extrovert nature.

RULER OF FIRST HOUSE IN FIFTH

These intelligent people are also sensually inclined. They may experience distresses in later years due to their children. They are good communicators.

RULER OF FIRST HOUSE IN SIXTH

During their lives these persons seem to have problems at every turn. They may be frequently sick and envious people also try to give them problems. However, on the positive side they can rise above and overcome such problems.

RULER OF FIRST HOUSE IN SEVENTH

These successful career people travel widely and communicate well. However, they may have problems with their chosen mate.

RULER OF FIRST HOUSE IN EIGHTH

Subjects have good intelligence and a capacity to gain much knowledge. They are sexually inclined, with desire for more than one partner, and may also often be sick, when young.

RULER OF FIRST HOUSE IN NINTH

Subjects tend to live good, clean lives, with many pleasures. Good communicators, they are also religiously inclined, with compassion for others.

RULER OF FIRST HOUSE IN TENTH

These good-looking people have self-confidence, set high goals for themselves and feel their work is extremely important. They achieve great success in their careers and may become well-known.

RULER OF FIRST HOUSE IN ELEVENTH

These are powerful and influential people who are very successful, with great gains in the career. They are satisfied people that achieve their goals and a high income.

RULER OF FIRST HOUSE IN TWELFTH

These persons, unsuccessful in their careers, turn to spirituality or philanthropic work. They may also suffer material losses.

RULER OF THE SECOND HOUSE

RULER OF SECOND HOUSE IN FIRST
Such people are somewhat crude in words and actions and, at times. lusty to the point of creating disturbances in the family. However, they are successful in business affairs.

RULER OF SECOND HOUSE IN SECOND
These people have many opportunities to satisfy their material desires. They may accumulate wealth and have a full love life, although the tendency is often for a small family. They may have a sharp tongue.

RULER OF SECOND HOUSE IN THIRD
These people are very materialistic, with little spiritual inclination. Consequently, they may tend to misuse the good intelligence with which they have been endowed.

RULER OF SECOND HOUSE IN FOURTH
These intelligent subjects may be particularly successful in property dealings and may inherit money from their mother.

RULER OF SECOND HOUSE IN FIFTH
Very sexually inclined, they may be cruel and materialistic subjects tending to use others to gain income and also have problems within the family group.

RULER OF SECOND HOUSE IN SIXTH
These sensual people tend to be involved with the underworld and, as a result suffer problems from the government. Others find their motives may be difficult to understand. They must guard their property from theft.

RULER OF SECOND HOUSE IN SEVENTH
These subjects may be doctors or nurses and often travel for business projects. They also tend to be unfaithful in marital relationships.

RULER OF SECOND HOUSE IN EIGHTH
Career success doesn't come easily to these people who have problems in communication with others, causing distress. Marriage may also be problematic, but, financially, could receive inheritance.

RULER OF SECOND HOUSE IN NINTH
These subjects may suffer sickness as a youth but later enjoy success in business and their career. They may be somewhat pious and gain knowledge in worthy subjects.

RULER OF SECOND HOUSE IN TENTH

Quite knowledgeable people but may be "full of themselves". They are good communicators with love for the opposite sex. They may be successful, especially in a career dealing with products that come from the earth.

RULER OF SECOND HOUSE IN ELEVENTH

A position which results in great success in both material and spiritual realms. Subjects make sound business partners and have a reliable group of social contacts. There is an inclination to physical pleasures.

RULER OF SECOND HOUSE IN TWELFTH

Generous to causes they believe in but outspoken and somewhat egotistical; these people do not make the best business associates, especially as they are willing to take risky cha.˙ ːes.

RULER OF THE THIRD HOUSE

RULER OF THIRD HOUSE IN FIRST

Subjects are often self-sufficient personalities and may also be boastful and showy. They tend toward anger and may become violent, if aroused.

RULER OF THIRD HOUSE IN SECOND

These people may be fairly good communicators but, do not have a lot of energy. They may also be involved in illegalities for profit.

RULER OF THIRD HOUSE IN THIRD

Subjects are prone to be forceful in both speech and actions. They may make money through the media. They are happy in life and there is harmony in the household.

RULER OF THIRD HOUSE IN FOURTH

Good, intelligent people who gain a fair measure of success. The marital partner may be unfaithful or, at times, do things which are upsetting.

RULER OF THIRD HOUSE IN FIFTH

Tends to cause those influenced to be sharp in business, with substantial monetary gains. However, they worry about their love lives. They may produce powerful offspring.

RULER OF THIRD HOUSE IN SIXTH

This influence results in indiscretion and misuse of intelligence when it comes to matters of the heart and career. They may also suffer from family problems.

RULER OF THIRD HOUSE IN SEVENTH

These people may have numerous problems with their mates and with many other people, due to their own actions. There is personal suffering when young.

RULER OF THIRD HOUSE IN EIGHTH

This is not a strong position for happiness or success in life. Subjects may have physical or mental problems and may earn through illegal means.

RULER OF THIRD HOUSE IN NINTH

This position often results in career advancement through a good marriage or partner. Subjects may be involved in communications. They may have a deep and solid relationship with a brother.

RULER OF THIRD HOUSE IN TENTH

This person is intelligent and a good communicator, with the drive to accomplish their goals in life. Their partner may be unfaithful. They may also have a famous brother.

RULER OF THIRD HOUSE IN ELEVENTH

This position produces powerful, self sufficient types, with strong will power. They may be showy or boastful, with a tendency towards anger.

RULER OF THIRD HOUSE IN TWELFTH

Subjects tend to have many ups and downs in life and may have substantial losses at times. They experience impermanent relationships with others and prefer solitude.

RULER OF THE FOURTH HOUSE

RULER OF FOURTH HOUSE IN FIRST

Subjects may be conscientious students and gain considerable knowledge from their studies. On the personal front there may be losses of family property, or separation of family members.

RULER OF FOURTH HOUSE IN SECOND

This position results in a successful person with good education and business acumen, who makes a good living. An achiever and goal setter who fulfils many desires and becomes satisfied with their living situation.

RULER OF FOURTH HOUSE IN THIRD

These people have the energy to accomplish what they set out to do. They have a strong physical constitution. Problems may stem from their spouse's family.

RULER OF FOURTH HOUSE IN FOURTH

These are intelligent and educated people who achieve success in careers or businesses dealing with real estate, automobiles, or machinery. They care for others and have good morals. Their mother is often considered a wonderful person.

RULER OF FOURTH HOUSE IN FIFTH

This situation results in subjects of great intelligence who may also be religious or philanthropic. Children may also make this person proud. May earn through real estate or property management.

RULER OF FOURTH HOUSE IN SIXTH

Subject may acquire debts and incur the wrath of others. They may be untrustworthy and unable to persevere, while having to learn to control their anger. They live far from their birthplace.

RULER OF FOURTH HOUSE IN SEVENTH

Such people are successful in real estate business and invest money wisely. They are very sensually inclined and their mate is an asset. There may be overseas travel.

RULER OF FOURTH HOUSE IN EIGHTH

This is not a good position for making profits on investments. Those so influenced may have mental agitation from being bothered by irrational people or, at times, from people who are completely insane. They may, as a child, lose or become separated from a parent.

RULER OF FOURTH HOUSE IN NINTH

This a beneficial placement that allows for both material and spiritual happiness. Subjects are intelligent and well educated, with many friends. They are helpful and enjoy learning new things.

RULER OF FOURTH HOUSE IN TENTH

This position results in conscientious people who are skilled in their work and who may profit from business involving real estate, automobiles, or machinery.

RULER OF FOURTH HOUSE IN ELEVENTH

This placement influences a subject to be an adept communicator who mixes well with groups and individuals alike. They wish for success in their endeavours and are usually successful.

RULER OF FOURTH HOUSE IN TWELFTH

This placement is not prone to giving material success or harmony in life. Material upheavals are common, making subjects more interested in spirituality.

RULER OF THE FIFTH HOUSE

RULER OF FIFTH HOUSE IN FIRST

This influence produces highly educated people whose opinions are valued. Their children may also be held in high regard. Generally they are most capable in their endeavours.

RULER OF FIFTH HOUSE IN SECOND

This situation produces very perceptive people who generally have a happy family life, adequate finances and tend to have large families.

RULER OF FIFTH HOUSE IN THIRD

Often this placement results in an intelligent person with a good birth and marital family. It may also result in having siblings who are successful in their chosen careers.

RULER OF FIFTH HOUSE IN FOURTH

This position produces an educated person with reliable friendships and a comfortable living situation. They are inclined to become involved in real estate business.

RULER OF FIFTH HOUSE IN FIFTH

This situation tends to result in an intelligent person who often meets with success through business in finance or entertainment. They may have anxiety over a member of their family, or child.

RULER OF FIFTH HOUSE IN SIXTH

This person is a materialist and has little interest in religion or spirituality. Children may cause mental distress or other problems.

RULER OF FIFTH HOUSE IN SEVENTH

Often results in a successful person with many noble qualities that endear them to others. An efficient and honest business person, with much to say. Children may be very successful.

RULER OF FIFTH HOUSE IN EIGHTH

This is not a calm or generally satisfied person. They are prone to fall into debt and have losses in their career. They may have problems in the lungs or chest area, and must learn to control their anger.

RULER OF FIFTH HOUSE IN NINTH

This tends to produce a successful person with a host of wonderful qualities, an excellent communicator with strong moral fibre. Children also tend to develop fine qualities.

RULER OF FIFTH HOUSE IN TENTH

Indicates a successful person who makes effective use of their time and money, rendering them financially stable. They tend to have friends in high places and their children will be successful.

RULER OF FIFTH HOUSE IN ELEVENTH

An appropriate placement for receiving a full education and being happy in life. A successful subject with many outstanding qualities. Children will also attain success.

RULER OF FIFTH HOUSE IN TWELFTH

This person may experience losses in the family and in the career as a result of this placement. A traveller who is spiritually inclined.

RULER OF THE SIXTH HOUSE

RULER OF SIXTH HOUSE IN FIRST

These people tend to gravitate towards living in a group or institution of some sort, far from their birthplace. They may also have health problems.

RULER OF SIXTH HOUSE IN SECOND

Those subject to the influence of this poor position are not particularly successful in their career or happy in the home situation and encounter difficulty in financial affairs. Physically there may be problems with eyesight and teeth.

RULER OF SIXTH HOUSE IN THIRD

These people tend to irritate others, due to a bad attitude and lack of respect. They need to control their anger. and may be somewhat artistic.

RULER OF SIXTH HOUSE IN FOURTH

Subjects have a dissatisfaction with their environment and general position in life which manifests itself in frequent relocation. People become upset about the instability of this person. They may also feel a lack of maternal love. There may be health problems in the chest area.

RULER OF SIXTH HOUSE IN FIFTH

Subjects may be successful in their business or career and enjoy the resulting opulence but must be careful of dealing in unrighteous businesses. They may spend time away from the family.

RULER OF SIXTH HOUSE IN SIXTH

Overseas travel and business in foreign places may become manifest for subjects who may also have abilities as healers.

RULER OF SIXTH HOUSE IN SEVENTH

These people may be successful in business, but unhappy with their sexual relationships. The spouse may be physically weak. Travel overseas, at various times, is indicated.

RULER OF SIXTH HOUSE IN EIGHTH

Subjects should be careful of getting into trouble or incurring losses due to the actions of others. Career difficulties are also indicated.

RULER OF SIXTH HOUSE IN NINTH

This position indicates that legal problems and difficulties with their father may arise. There may be frequent travel overseas, for business or pleasure.

RULER OF SIXTH HOUSE IN TENTH
This person has a difficult time making advancement in their career. Poor discretion may be there and they may make enemies.

RULER OF SIXTH HOUSE IN ELEVENTH
Powerful people, with highly placed friends, that meet with success. However, they are considerate of the needs and desires of other people.

RULER OF SIXTH HOUSE IN TWELFTH
Subjects are not of strong mental or physical constitution and must learn regulation in their lives or they may easily become ill. They may have philosophical interests.

RULER OF THE SEVENTH HOUSE

RULER OF SEVENTH HOUSE IN FIRST
Subjects find much energy expended in their occupation. They may be a traveller or do business requiring some travel, and are considerate of their spouse.

RULER OF SEVENTH HOUSE IN SECOND
Subjects are financially secure but are too preoccupied with sexual relationships and other sensual pleasures. Health may be adversely affected due to overconsumption. They should learn moderation and develop spiritual interests.

RULER OF SEVENTH HOUSE IN THIRD
This position tends towards a powerful or overpowering person. Nevertheless, they will mix well with others. They may experience loss of a child.

RULER OF SEVENTH HOUSE IN FOURTH
This tends to produce intelligent people who progress to higher education. Gains a wonderful spouse and enjoys adequate financial prosperity while working for the benefit of many others.

RULER OF SEVENTH HOUSE IN FIFTH
This is a very good position. Subjects are fortunate in marriage, children and their career. They may become rich and could work in the entertainment industry.

RULER OF SEVENTH HOUSE IN SIXTH
Not a good position for marital happiness. Subjects may contract sexually transmitted diseases and/or be unhappy in their love life.

RULER OF SEVENTH HOUSE IN SEVENTH
These people tend to be inspirational, having bright ideas and making for success in business or the career. They have communicative abilities and are also "lucky in love".

RULER OF SEVENTH HOUSE IN EIGHTH
An unfavourable position whereby subjects have problems with their love lives and indeed their marriage partner may commit illegal acts, landing them in prison, or may suffer an early death. Subjects also have difficulties in their career, but do have an interest in philosophy. They may die far from their birthplace.

RULER OF SEVENTH HOUSE IN NINTH
This good position makes for a wealthy or powerful person who is happy with their spouse and successful in their career, which may involve fruitful travels.

RULER OF SEVENTH HOUSE IN TENTH

This generally produces a person who predominates over others, is successful in both the career and marriage and makes a reliable business partner.

RULER OF SEVENTH HOUSE IN ELEVENTH

Such people may become wealthy, influential and successful in their career. Generally the spouse's family is "high-class".

RULER OF SEVENTH HOUSE IN TWELFTH

These people suffer setbacks in business and may lose their marriage partner due to different reasons. They are not always comfortable around others. Mentally they may be preoccupied with sex and need to try to divest themselves of this obsession for spiritual progress.

RULER OF THE EIGHTH HOUSE

RULER OF EIGHTH HOUSE IN FIRST

Subjects may be spiritually inclined but suffer many failures in business and in their love life. Physical health is poor and they are often indiscreet in what they may voice to others.

RULER OF EIGHTH HOUSE IN SECOND

Many losses are incurred by those with this placement. They must learn to speak more kindly about and to others They may also engage in illegal business for profit.

RULER OF EIGHTH HOUSE IN THIRD

This person must learn to become more kindly disposed to others. There may be a loss of physical and/or mental energy and problems within the family.

RULER OF EIGHTH HOUSE IN FOURTH

Those influenced have an unstable family life, when young. They tend to waste their money and may have ignoble desires. Need to learn more self-control.

RULER OF EIGHTH HOUSE IN FIFTH

This usually results in a capable, compassionate person who generally has few siblings and/or children. In fact a child may go away, or suffer early death. Physically there can be digestion problems.

RULER OF EIGHTH HOUSE IN SIXTH

Subjects tend to find dissatisfaction with job or career. They are generally of a weak physical constitution and may be preyed upon by cheats or thieves.

RULER OF EIGHTH HOUSE IN SEVENTH

Business advancement may often prove to be difficult for these people who may also divorce, due to the intolerable personality or actions of their spouse.

RULER OF EIGHTH HOUSE IN EIGHTH

This position produces a very influential person, who may live to a ripe old age and get an inheritance, but may have some unbecoming inclinations which should be guarded against.

RULER OF EIGHTH HOUSE IN NINTH

This undisciplined person has problems in both the birth and marriage family. They may also suffer losses in relation to people once close to them.

RULER OF EIGHTH HOUSE IN TENTH

This position tends to produce capable people, yet difficulties arise in their career and success may be evasive. They may get inheritance from the family. Physically they should be careful of back problems.

RULER OF EIGHTH HOUSE IN ELEVENTH

Eccentricities may be present in the personality of these people but they still make good friends. Physically they may experience pain in the ears.

RULER OF EIGHTH HOUSE IN TWELFTH

Not a favourable position for success or fulfilment in the career and financial affairs are generally weak. However such people do have the positive feature of spiritual awareness.

RULER OF THE NINTH HOUSE

RULER OF NINTH HOUSE IN FIRST
This position tends to produce happy and generous people with many fine qualities. They are contented, philosophical and dutiful.

RULER OF NINTH HOUSE IN SECOND
These people meet with success in both material and spiritual spheres of life. They make financial and material gains and have excellent communicative abilities.

RULER OF NINTH HOUSE IN THIRD
Born as good communicators, these people tend to rise out of their family social class. They have a pleasant disposition and are fairly successful in their careers.

RULER OF NINTH HOUSE IN FOURTH
This position usually leads to a successful career person. They may be property owners and lead a full social life.

RULER OF NINTH HOUSE IN FIFTH
These are intelligent, capable people whose opinions are of value and who enjoy success and prosperity in both the birth and marital family.

RULER OF NINTH HOUSE IN SIXTH
This position causes many difficulties in career advancement but, with perseverance, success can be had to some degree. There may be disagreements within the family.

RULER OF NINTH HOUSE IN SEVENTH
Persons with this placement meet with success and happiness. They are able to achieve what they desire, get a nice spouse and have both material prosperity, as well as spiritual fulfilment.

RULER OF NINTH HOUSE IN EIGHTH
This position often results in a lonely and frustrated person. They may lose their father when young and may deal in illegal businesses.

RULER OF NINTH HOUSE IN NINTH
This person is blessed with many noble qualities. They are great communicators and may be inspirational to others. They are religious and also successful in career and gaining wealth.

RULER OF NINTH HOUSE IN TENTH

This is a position for success in the career, wealth, good friends, education and sensibility.

RULER OF NINTH HOUSE IN ELEVENTH

This is a successful person with many opportunities to enjoy life. Reliable friends are gained, along with financial prosperity.

RULER OF NINTH HOUSE IN TWELFTH

These unselfish people are hard, steady workers but may have problems with their superiors at times. They are caring and have spiritual interests.

RULER OF THE TENTH HOUSE

RULER OF TENTH HOUSE IN FIRST

This situation produces an adept communicator and very capable person who can accomplish things impossible for most. They have desires to help the general population by their actions.

RULER OF TENTH HOUSE IN SECOND

Powerful and wealthy people who may enjoy success in their family's business, or may often be jewellers, restauranteurs or merchants in produce.

RULER OF TENTH HOUSE IN THIRD

These people may be powerful and energetic. Usually they are well-educated and possess humanitarian desires. Family ties are strong especially with brothers and their own children.

RULER OF TENTH HOUSE IN FOURTH

Subjects tend to be well-mannered, educated people that are greatly respected and popular with others. The facility for material gains is good.

RULER OF TENTH HOUSE IN FIFTH

This is a fortunate placement, indicating wealth and prosperity and children may also be very successful. A career in the entertainment industry is a possibility.

RULER OF TENTH HOUSE IN SIXTH

This position usually puts subjects in a service position with mediocre gains. There is a tendency to be underhanded for profit.

RULER OF TENTH HOUSE IN SEVENTH

A fortunate situation which results in success in life, both business and marital. Excellent communicators who may attain to some measure of fame.

RULER OF TENTH HOUSE IN EIGHTH

A difficult position and subjects should be wary of influences. They may be inclined to engage in harmful activities that can land them in jail. They may end up as a spiritualist with no material accomplishments to speak of. It is also not a sound influence for professional success.

RULER OF TENTH HOUSE IN NINTH

This is an excellent placement for success in all endeavours. These popular people enjoy family life, advancement in career and may wield considerable influence.

RULER OF TENTH HOUSE IN TENTH

These subjects are very successful in their career and perform noble works. They tend to befriend highly-placed and influential associates and may attain an influential position, becoming famous as a result. They may also receive a family inheritance.

RULER OF TENTH HOUSE IN ELEVENTH

Those so influenced benefit from good family ties and also get much enjoyment and sense gratification in life. They may be rich, powerful and important to the success of others.

RULER OF TENTH HOUSE IN TWELFTH

Not a good position for material or career advancement but they may be spiritually inclined. Subjects may act in negative ways in all spheres of life and should strive to overcome this with a more positive attitude.

RULER OF THE ELEVENTH HOUSE

RULER OF ELEVENTH HOUSE IN FIRST

A position for opportunity, especially in relation to money, friends and material pleasures.

RULER OF ELEVENTH HOUSE IN SECOND

A position which tends to produce subjects with excellent capabilities for wealth and success and, consequently, may enjoy a luxurious lifestyle. They could have particular success in partnership businesses.

RULER OF ELEVENTH HOUSE IN THIRD

These people are good communicators that can influence others. They have kind relatives and may take a career in the art world.

RULER OF ELEVENTH HOUSE IN FOURTH

This is a strong placement for the fulfilment of material desires. Money may be gained through land or real estate transactions or an inheritance. They tend to have influential friends.

RULER OF ELEVENTH HOUSE IN FIFTH

This influence tends to produce an educated and good-hearted person. They usually have small families. In business they may gamble on unusual ventures, which may reap high returns.

RULER OF ELEVENTH HOUSE IN SIXTH

Subjects may feel uncomfortable in public or situations of prominence but while they may be argumentative, they excel in supportive roles.

RULER OF ELEVENTH HOUSE IN SEVENTH

These people are attractive to the opposite sex and have strong sensual desires. There are mutual gains made by such relationships, especially involving success in overseas business.

RULER OF ELEVENTH HOUSE IN EIGHTH

An unfortunate placement whereby subjects tend to suffer material losses, lack of friends or mate and are generally shortlived.

RULER OF ELEVENTH HOUSE IN NINTH

This is an excellent placement. Subjects are generous, religious and may be involved with charitable organizations. They have many friends, pleasures and opulences.

RULER OF ELEVENTH HOUSE IN TENTH

These are influential and humanitarian people who are successful in undertakings.

RULER OF ELEVENTH HOUSE IN ELEVENTH

This is another good placement resulting in easy money and the capacity to attain opulence, friendships and enjoyments in life. However, subjects should strive towards some spiritual progress while enjoying the material side.

RULER OF ELEVENTH HOUSE IN TWELFTH

Subjects may endure many material losses. They may also lose their marriage partner, friends and unhealthy activities may shorten their own life span However there will, more than likely, be spiritual progress.

RULER OF THE TWELFTH HOUSE

RULER OF TWELFTH HOUSE IN FIRST

Not a strong placement as subjects tend to be of weak physical constitution with unusual habits. However they may also be spiritually inclined and make progress in this area.

RULER OF TWELFTH HOUSE IN SECOND

These are generous and compassionate people who may be religious or philosophical. Physically they have weak vision.

RULER OF TWELFTH HOUSE IN THIRD

The influence of this placement causes problems for those who are ruled by it. Subjects tend to act with ill intent toward other people and their family, causing them to break these bonds.

RULER OF TWELFTH HOUSE IN FOURTH

This is another placement in which to exercise caution. Subjects have a tendency to be restless, unfaithful and generally anti-social. They tend to concentrate on material possessions, rather than spiritual and karmic results.

RULER OF TWELFTH HOUSE IN FIFTH

A good placement for religious education and development but may be unsuccessful in business. Subjects may suffer losses in the area of children and feel, at times, unfulfilled in general.

RULER OF TWELFTH HOUSE IN SIXTH

These are good-looking generous people who may spend time overseas. They may have legal problems at times and suffer other difficulties through actions of the spouse.

RULER OF TWELFTH HOUSE IN SEVENTH

Although these people are spiritually inclined, they have poor discretionary powers and may, at times, be bothered by people who would be better avoided. There is enjoyment from considerable travel.

RULER OF TWELFTH HOUSE IN EIGHTH

A good situation giving rise to a generous and upright person, religious and philosophical in attitude and respected due to the magnanimous treatment of those less fortunate. There should be spiritual advancement as a result, if the opportunities are used.

RULER OF TWELFTH HOUSE IN NINTH

A placement with some difficulties in that the father is not helpful. Subjects may be perceived as being arrogant, causing difficulties with those in authority. Lack of self discipline is also a tendency.

RULER OF TWELFTH HOUSE IN TENTH

Although this position causes material losses and lack of successes in the career these are philosophical people who can take things in their stride. They are particularly effective in supportive capacities and should concentrate on this role.

RULER OF TWELFTH HOUSE IN ELEVENTH

These people are excitable, highly-strung and very sexually oriented, expending much energy and money in that direction. They should guard against such energy-draining influences.

RULER OF TWELFTH HOUSE IN TWELFTH

A wonderful placement that indicates a kind and religious person who spends money wisely and enjoys travel to far-away places.

INTERPRETATION OF THE CHART AND PREDICTING THE FUTURE

To understand what events may occur, as well as other influences on emotions, intelligence, actions, etc. we look at various factors. There are many different factors to take into account when interpreting the horoscope. There is a system of planetary periods in vedic astrology which allows prediction when the influences of particular planets will be dominant and what results may be expected during these times. We are always in the major planetary period of some planet. When a vedic astrologer casts a chart this information is also provided, with exact dates as to when the various planetary periods begin and end. During each major planetary period there is also a sub-period for each planet.

The length of the major planetary periods are from six to twenty years, depending on which planet, as they all have different lengths to their major periods. The length of the major period is divided into nine (unequal parts) and each of these becomes a sub-period of one of the planets. For instance, the major period of Jupiter lasts sixteen years. In the first two years+ the major period is Jupiter and the sub-period is also Jupiter. Therefore we would call that period Jupiter-Jupiter. Then comes the Saturn sub-period for some time and that period would be called Jupiter-Saturn and so on, until all planets have ruled a sub-period through to the end of the sixteen year period.

Having determined the major period, we look at the house ruled. In the case of Jupiter it is the ruler of both Sagittarius and Pisces. Therefore we look to see how well Jupiter is situated. This is by its placement in sign and house, which will give us the general quality of its influence and what areas of life are ruled by these houses. In our example horoscope, (see overleaf) Sagittarius is the ascendant, or rising sign. Therefore Jupiter rules the first house (the ascendant), as well as the fourth house, as it is the ruler of Sagittarius (first) and Pisces (fourth). Jupiter is a natural benefic of the highest order and also a temporary benefic, as Sagittarius is rising. This makes it an extremely powerful force for good in this horoscope. It is conjunct with Venus in the sixth house, giving some of the qualities of Venus in its own sign, Taurus, also by association. Jupiter is ruler of the first house in the sixth and also ruler of the fourth house in the sixth. In its sixth house position, Jupiter is receiving no other aspects from other planets, so considering house position, sign position, lordships (houses it rules) and the effects of being conjunct with Venus, we get a good understanding of how Jupiter is influencing this chart.*

See planetary aspects at the end of this chapter.

Then we look to the "chandra lagna" chart, which is simply making the house where the Moon is the first house (in this case it would be Capricorn, presently the second house,) and judge the chart in the same way from that angle. Jupiter is a very benefic influence in our sample chart, both in the birth chart and the chandra lagna (placing the house with the Moon as the first house). There are influences concerning children, as Jupiter takes the fifth house from the Moon. There are many obstacles and some mental unrest, judging from its position in the birth chart, but also great strength to overcome any difficulties in life. We must consider that Jupiter's nature here is powerful to do good and we must also look to the categories of life Jupiter rules, regardless of its placement in the chart.

It aspects the second house (accumulation of money, experiences in family life, speech, diet, etc.) and the tenth house (career, status, etc.), so during the Jupiter major period there will be a rise in status, accumulation of funds, a chance to speak publicly and a good diet. As the sixth house represents travel, foreign countries, enemies, service, etc. there will be success in foreign places, quite a bit of travelling internationally, a chance to serve God and fellow man and no enemies will succeed against him.

Now looking to the "navamsa" chart, we see that Jupiter is in the fourth house conjunct Venus and Mars in Leo (see sample chart). This position must be considered in the same way as we did in the birth chart and chandra lagna according to house and sign position, rulership (in this case Jupiter rules the eighth and eleventh houses), aspects (only aspected by Rahu in Aries from its twelfth house position) and gain an understanding of its influences from that angle.

There are sixteen subdivisional charts that may be used to gain an understanding of more subtle influences, although they are extremely difficult to understand, especially for the novice. The most important are the navamsa and the chandra lagna, already mentioned above. Shown in the navamsa are the marital affairs of this lifetime and, more importantly, it can show the "condition" of the soul in its passing from birth to birth. This is something which takes much experience, as well as spiritual progress in the astrologer's life, to properly understand.

Remember that in judging the overall significance or strength of the whole horoscope we first judge the strength of the most important and significant ascendant sign, the Moon and the ninth house which are factors. The most auspicious houses in the chart are the first, fourth, seventh and tenth, called "angles", "kendras" or "quadrants" and the "trines", which are the first, fifth, and ninth houses. It is best to have benefics situated in these most important houses.

The sixth, eighth, and twelfth houses are considered malefic houses and it's actually good to have malefic planets here, rather than in "angles" or "trines", where they can cause more problems.

Finally there are also different "yogas", or combinations of planets, that suggest different levels and varieties of enjoyment, or suffering. I am not going into detail in this introductory book on all of these,but they are extremely important in evaluation of a chart, so much so, that good yogas can nullify negative implications in the chart and bad yogas can nullify positive ones. It is important to learn these yogas to enable you to recognize them, when evaluating a horoscope. The most important yoga for power and influence is known as a "raja-yoga". Raja means king and yoga means combination, so this is a "kingly combination", capable of bestowing great wealth, enjoyment, career potential, etc., depending on the house the raja-yoga occurs in. It is caused by the ruler (lord) of an "angle" and the ruler of a "trine" combining influences in some way. This could be either by being conjunct or both aspecting a particular house.

There are other important yogas:-

A/ Examples of benefic yogas;

"Shubhakartari -yoga" which occurs if benefic planets surround a planet or a house, increasing the potency or categories respectively, in a positive way.

"Dhurdhura" yoga results when benefics surround the Moon.

"Obhayachari-yoga" results when benefics surround the Sun.

"Hamsa-yoga" a great yoga for enjoying life in many ways, results when Jupiter is in its own sign, or exalted in an "angle".

"Malavya-yoga" is similar, occurring when Venus is in its own sign, or exalted in an "angle".

"Bhadra-yoga" occurs when Mercury is in its own or exaltation sign in an angle, indicating great intellect and communicative abilities.

"Ruchaka-yoga" occurs when Mars is in its own or exaltation sign in an angle giving great energy, leadership ability and success in areas of life ruled by Mars.

"Sasi-yoga" occurs when Saturn is in its own or exaltation sign in an angle allowing a long life span and a person to become extremely influential over others.

B/ Examples of malefic yogas;

"Papakarti-yoga" occurs if malefic planets surround a planet or a house, afflicting it and decreasing its effect. Having the rulers of the first, fifth, ninth and tenth houses in the sixth, eighth or twelfth houses causes malefic results also.

"Kemadruma-yoga" occurs when no planets are on either side of the Moon or no benefic planets aspecting it. The result is, unfortunately, a lonely life.

"Kalasarpa-yoga" results when all the planets are situated in between Rahu and Ketu. This indicates suffering - possibly as a result of a curse in the previous life, or simply misfortune.

"Sakata-yoga" occurs when the Moon is in the sixth, eighth or twelfth house from Jupiter. It generally causes disparity in life. Sometimes the native will have much more material facility than is necessary and at other times feel bereft of good luck.

C/ A yoga called "mutual reception or "Parivarthana-yoga" occurs when two planets are situated in each other's signs. If Mars was in Virgo and Mercury in Aries, this would be an example of this yoga, as Mercury owns Virgo, where Mars is situated and Mars owns Aries, where Mercury is situated. This strengthens and enhances the energies of the two planets involved. To understand if this is positive or negative, we need to consider all factors like the natural and temporary nature of the planets involved, the houses they are in, aspects they receive, etc.

One other difficulty in planetary positions is called "combustion". This is when a planet is too close to the Sun. This results in its energies being "burned up", so to speak, rendering it weak or too impotent to give beneficial results. There are exact degrees for each planet being in "combustion" but a general "rule of thumb" is that if a planet is within five degrees of the sun, it becomes combust. Mercury and Venus are both normally close to the Sun, so would be less affected.

This list of yogas is by no means complete. I would direct readers to a book called "Three Hundred Important Combinations" by B.V. Raman for information on yogas and their influences.

With all of these various influences combined, we can then make predictions during the major period. We then look to the minor period, and whatever influences connected with the planet ruling the sub-period will combine with the influences of the planet ruling the major period. (See sample).

Transits of planets through the stars and signs also has an effect on our daily lives. According to the birth chart, the influences will vary. Your astrologer should also give this information when doing your horoscope. In the interest of keeping this book simple, so more people will be inclined to read it, as well as understand it, I am not giving specific information on how to calculate the planetary transits.

Thus, to predict the future, all the various influences combined in the chart lead to conclusions. It is an incredibly accurate science but it takes a learned astrologer with experience, as well as good powers of intuition, to interpret and predict correctly. However, if a particular result reoccurs through different influences in the chart, then you can assume it is conclusive.

As with all things, the more you practice interpreting charts, as well as increasing your knowledge through study, the more adept you will become in this great science. If you master the principles in this book, understanding them thoroughly, you will find an advanced study of books from India more useful as, generally they are written for those that already have some knowledge and experience with vedic astrology.

To give some useful generalizations on different categories of life look to the strength (or weakness) of:-

> Sun and the first house to determine a person's character;
> Jupiter and the second house for an ability to save or accumulate money and/or opulence;
> Mars and the third house for determination of talents;
> Moon and fourth house for affairs relating to your mother;
> Venus and the fourth house to determine affairs relating to the home, automobiles, etc;
> Jupiter and the fifth house for affairs to do with children;
> Sun, first, and sixth houses to judge health;
> Jupiter and the sixth house for looking at legal problems (or the lack of);
> Venus and the seventh house for marriage or love life;
> Mercury and the seventh for business affairs;
> Saturn and the eighth for duration of life;
> Jupiter, Venus, Moon, Mercury and the ninth house for spiritual inclinations;
> Saturn, Mars, Mercury, and the tenth house for career;
> Jupiter, Venus, and the eleventh house for gains of all types;
> Twelfth house for an indication of future birth.

Having your horoscope done will, hopefully, instill a desire to perform positive actions to, not only reduce bad karma in this lifetime, but to create a better future. The knowledge to shape our destinies positively, both materially and spiritually, is something each and every one of us should aspire to obtain. In this way we can become the masters of our own destinies by performing positive actions in full knowledge of the results.

PLANETARY ASPECTS

Planets influence specific houses according to their position. They cast partial and full aspects but we are only going to be concerned with the full aspects here. Most astrologers only consider the full aspects to be of paramount importance in evaluation, anyway.

The aspects are considered to be cast a certain number of houses ahead of it, counting the house that the planet resides in as the first. The aspects are cast in a forward (ahead) direction only, never backwards. The aspects for each planet are:

SUN......................seventh house ahead
MOON...................seventh house ahead
MARS....................fourth, seventh and eighth houses ahead
MERCURY.............seventh house ahead
JUPITER................fifth, seventh, and ninth houses ahead
VENUS..................seventh house ahead
SATURN................third, seventh, and tenth houses ahead
RAHU....................fifth, seventh, and ninth houses ahead
KETU....................fifth, seventh, and ninth houses ahead

"Aspect" means the planet casts an influence according to its natural nature, temporary nature, sign and house position, association with other planets, etc. Therefore, in deciding if an aspect is positive or negative, as well as what traits it carries with it, it is necessary to carefully study the position and influences surrounding the aspecting planet.

Aspects are extremely important and must be considered in the interpretation of the chart. They are such powerful factors that "raja yoga" can be made by mutual aspects on a particular house by the rulers of a "quadrant" (first, fourth, seventh and tenth houses) and a "trine" (first, fifth, and ninth houses).

MAIN POINTS FROM PART TWO

1/ There are nine planets, representing various energies in life. They influence the horoscope for better or worse, depending on various factors, including the aspect they cast on the twelve houses.

2/ The twelve signs of the zodiac give a general idea of the qualities of those born within their influence.

3/ The twelve houses denote areas of life with which people will be concerned. The signs are placed within them in strict natural order following the rising sign which is placed in the first house.

4/ The rising sign is most important in relation to the personality of those born under its influence.

5/ Planets in the signs and houses exert powerful influences. A description of signs ruled, and positions gives details of the influences felt.

6/ The "Nakshtra" or "star" chart, gives more precise detail of specific traits within the signs.

7/ Planets also have "temporary" influences, dependant upon the rising sign. Descriptions of these influences were listed.

8/ Lordship of signs is also very important for interpretation of traits their influences produce.

9/ Having listed all the relevant categories a chart can be interpreted by those so trained. For the novice conclusions can only be safely made if the same outcomes/traits are shown from each of the influences. An example horoscope is included and used to work through as an interpretation.

PART THREE

REMEDIAL MEASURES, SUCCESSFUL PROGRESS AND CONCLUSION

REMEDIAL MEASURES IN ASTROLOGY

Once an astrologer has done the horoscope it is their job to help you to balance influences within it to achieve greater harmony, success and satisfaction in all areas of life. Remember that this science should be used practically in order to help you deal with all facets of life presently and in the future. It should not just be a mystical curiosity with no practical utility. There are different remedial measures to be offered through vedic astrology.

AUSTERITIES

In theory there are particular austerities that one can perform to alleviate the effects of negative karma and there are vedic sacrifices that can also be performed to this end. These two means are extremely difficult to enact in this day and age, as severe austerities and penances are almost impossible for most of us and the vedic sacrifices require priests (brahmans), expert in chanting the vedic mantras, to gain the desired result. There are almost no brahmans today expert in this science that can be engaged for this purpose and, especially in the West, they are not to be found. Therefore these two remedial measures are difficult at best.

CHARITY

Another remedial measure is the act of giving, to worthy recipients. An expert astrologer, in knowledge of correct spiritual principles in this regard, can give recommendations for this. Every action has a reaction in some way, shape or form. To give in charity to worthy recipients, such as God conscious persons engaged in true spiritual welfare work, gives beneficial results to a fantastic degree. Giving to help those less fortunate in foodstuffs, shelter, medical care, etc. will also bring positive reactions. By the same token, giving to unworthy causes brings no positive reaction and may implicate you in the negative actions performed, due to the facility given by the act of, so-called, charity. A simple example is that if you give a homeless person liquor, or money that will be used to purchase liquor, no good reaction will be gained by the giving of such charity. If you give food to a hungry person, help them with medical treatment, etc., this is pious and will bring a positive reaction.

MANTRAS

These can be chanted to propitiate ill effects caused by weak or malefic planets. I will not list them all here but my feeling is that the greatest benefit can be gained by chanting mantras for purely spiritual benefit and that time is better utilized in this manner. Planetary mantras will help certain areas of life in regards to only this one birth. The mantras of "Vishnu Sahastranam" (the thousand names of Vishnu) can help in attaining higher levels of knowledge and spiritual consciousness which is not finished at the time of death, or transference of the soul from the present body.

There are many different mantras, such as "Om Namo Shivaya" (to Shiva), "Om Shanti Shanti Shanti" (a transcendental mantra for bringing about peace) and "Aum" (Omkara, the transcendental vibration). Through personal practice and experience, as well as through study and instruction, my feeling and realization is that the mantra given as the means for self realization in this age by Sri Chaitanya Mahaprabhu, in India 500 years ago, gives the most obvious results. This mantra, chanted throughout India, has been introduced in the West in the last few decades. It is the Hare Krishna maha-mantra. (Maha means "great", in a spiritual sense.) It is chanted as; "Hare Krishna Hare Krishna Krishna Krishna Hare Hare Hare Rama Hare Rama Rama Rama Hare Hare".

Some vedic mantras need absolute perfection in the pronunciation and meter of the chanting, requiring great expertise on the part of the practitioner, yet this Hare Krishna maha-mantra is said to be so powerful (invoking the original names of the supreme personality of Godhead) that, even chanted incorrectly,the benefit will be realized.

The timeless wisdom delineating the nature of matter and spirit and what activities are necessary for spiritual realization, are perfectly presented in "Bhagavad-Gita As It Is", by His Divine Grace A.C. Bhaktivedanta Swami Prabhupada. This version of the great epic is accepted by scholars to be the only authorized translation in English available here in the West. It has also been translated into many other languages. Bhaktivedanta Swami presented such a perfect and true rendition of this great literary work that it is used as a text in universities throughout the world in sanskrit, philosophy and religion departments. I would urge anyone unfamiliar with his work to obtain a copy, which should be available in any large bookstore.

In addition to mantras, there are yantras, or planetary symbols, that may be used to propitiate the negative effects of certain planets in the horoscope. There are two types, geometric and mathematical. Geometric yantras are specific designs that require someone with the talent to reproduce them properly on paper board, or on copper. Mathematical yantras are based on mathematical configurations of numbers which also have potency to propitiate negative effects of stellar influences.

Finally there is gemstone therapy, which, although utilized since ancient times to the present day in India and much of the East, is now gaining popularity and interest in the West. As it is extremely powerful and is of great interest. I will fully explain its use.

GEMSTONE THERAPY

I was brought up in the gemstone business from a young age and it was on a trip to India as a teenager that I was taught the astrological usage of gems, leading me to further study of this great and holy science of astrology.

Gem therapy, or planetary gemology, dates back to ancient Indian, Greek, Egyptian and Jewish cultures. Men and women would wear gems for the potencies imparted, not for their monetary value. Kings and queens would wear gemstones in their crowns and elsewhere on the body as a means of expanding their influence throughout the kingdom. Of course, the gems royalty wore were extremely large and of the highest quality to have such effects but gems may be utilized by the populace at large for beneficial effects in life.

The Vedic scriptures of ancient India contain the most complete descriptions and scientific knowledge of gemstones. They give specific details about various gems' potencies as well as prescriptions for their proper medical and astrological usage. In ancient cultures gems became the basis for directing the subtle forces of nature. The properties of gems have also been recognized in modern technology, as in quartz crystals in time pieces and diamonds in lasers and supercomputers. As a matter of fact over a billion people in the world today have taken advantage of planetary gemology to enhance their lives physically, mentally and spiritually. Only in the West does this seem to be "New Age". In Eastern countries it has been known for thousands of years, dating back to earliest recorded times.

Planetary gemology is based on the ancient system of sidereal astrology, the extremely accurate and enlightening system utilizing fixed positions of stars and constellations already described earlier in this book.. This system is very precise in determining strengths, weaknesses and destiny. The positions of the planets, at the time of our birth, reflect the karma that we bring with us into this life from our past actions and experiences. They represent the multitude of energies in the universe, each planet controlling a different form of cosmic energy which is transmitted throughout the solar system. These transmissions of energy are responsible for formations of life on this planet, including our bodies and minds.

The orbiting planets receive and give specific wave lengths of energy, which maintain the order of the solar system. These energies are transmitted as light. Another name for astrology is "Jyotish", or the "science of light". There are seven basic cosmic rays emanated by the seven major planets, Sun, Moon, Mars, Mercury, Jupiter, Venus, and Saturn. The signs of the zodiac and the different houses in the astrological horoscope represent the different fields that the planetary energies react and move within, thereby giving us information of how these energies will let us "read" what our life experiences will be in this incarnation. We are able to understand the quality of this birth in the same way as the nature of a tree can be read from the seed it is born from. This karma is what will determine how our lives will manifest themselves. The system of remedial measures in vedic astrology allows you to increase these energies vibrated from certain planets to balance and bring harmony. The two most practical utilize sound vibration, as in the chanting of mantras and increasing the vibrations of light, which is the basis for gemstone therapy.

Different gemstones, transmitters of electromagnetic energy, receive their potencies from the cosmic energies of different planets, thereby having different effects on the wearer. They do this by absorption and reflection of light frequencies. The electromagnetic energy emanating from the gemstone reacts with the similar energy of the body to produce certain effects. Which gemstones should be used must be determined through careful analysis of the astrological horoscope. The "New Age" practice of indiscriminately placing gemstone crystals all over the body can be extremely dangerous if the practitioner is not well-versed in this science. Gem crystals are very powerful and, as easily as they can positively enforce electromagnetic fields of the body, they can disrupt them giving the opposite effect. This can cause physical and mental debilities, so exercise extreme caution. Used incorrectly there can be disturbances on a subtle, astral level, as well as a physical one. Used correctly they can give a lift and greater potency in our lives in many ways, physically, mentally and spiritually.

Once you have had a careful analysis of your horoscope, by a vedic astrologer, the correct stone may then be set in a ring, or pendant, so that the stone comes into contact with the skin. This allows the gems to best transmit these frequencies of light or electromagnetic energy to the cells in our bodies. This is done through ions. The reason the fingers are the best place to wear gems is the location of many nerve centres there. I have seen amazing results in people's lives through gemstone therapy.

However, a word of caution, in order to be effective, gems must be natural (not synthetic) and untreated by excessive heat or irradiation to improve their appearance. This is often done in the jewellry trade for commercial purposes. This is not deceptive, unless a jeweller does not disclose the fact that the gem has been enhanced. Therefore, you must be certain that the source for your purchase has untreated gems. I have had the unenviable task, at times, of explaining to a client that, although the gem which they purchased is beautiful, as well as costly, it has no effect on the planetary energies, nor on their person, except as a form of colour therapy alone. (This science of colour therapy was derived from the ancient science of gemstone therapy.) It is not necessary to spend a fortune to obtain a gem that will give one the desired effects and the wonderful thing about utilizing the potency of gemstones is that it is a one-time cost. Its potency will never diminish and you have the gem for a lifetime.

GEMSTONES FOR EACH PLANET

SUN: RUBY (SUBSTITUTE IS RED GARNET)

MOON: PEARL (SUBSTITUTE IS MOONSTONE)

MARS: RED CORAL (SUBSTITUTE IS RED JASPER)

MERCURY: EMERALD OR GREEN JADE (SUBSTITUTE IS PERIDOT)

JUPITER: YELLOW SAPPHIRE
(SUBSTITUTE IS YELLOW TOPAZ OR CITRINE)

VENUS: DIAMOND (SUBSTITUTE IS TURQUOISE)

SATURN: BLUE SAPPHIRE
(SUBSTITUTE IS AMETHYST OR LAPIS LAZULI)

Note: The primary gemstones for all the planets, except Mars, should weigh at least 2 carats. For Mars, the red coral should weigh 8 carats, as should the substitute red jasper. The substitute gemstones should weigh at least 5 carats to have proper potency.

Further information on planetary gemology, and astrological uses of gems may be found in my book, "Gemstone Therapy for the Modern Age", which also describes the origin and usefulness of the original astrological birthstone system. It should be noted that the birthstone system in use today in the West is a bogus system, having no use other than for jewellers to sell specific gemstones to their customers. It was created in about 1917 by several jewellry organizations in the United States.

ASTROLOGICAL BIRTHSTONE SYSTEM

GEMSTONE	ASTROLOGICAL SIGN	ARIES	TAURUS	GEMINI	CANCER	LEO	VIRGO	LIBRA	SCORPIO	SAGITTARIUS	CAPRICORN	AQUARIUS	PISCES
	WESTERN or TROPICAL	March 21 to April 19	April 20 to May 20	May 21 to June 20	June 21 to July 22	July 23 to Aug. 22	Aug. 23 to Sept. 22	Sept. 23 to Oct. 22	Oct. 23 to Nov. 21	Nov. 22 to Dec. 21	Dec. 22 to Jan. 19	Jan. 20 to Feb. 18	Feb 19 to March 20
	EASTERN or SIDEREAL	April 14 to May 13	May 14 to June 13	June 14 to July 15	July 16 to Aug. 15	Aug. 16 to Sept. 15	Sept. 16 to Oct. 15	Oct. 17 to Nov. 15	Nov. 16 to Dec. 14	Dec. 15 to Jan. 13	Jan. 14 to Feb. 12	Feb. 13 to March 13	March 14 to April 13
GEMSTONES		Red Coral or Jasper	Diamond or White Topaz	Emerald or Green Jade	Pearl or Moonstone	Ruby or Red Tourmaline	Emerald or Green Jade	Diamond or White Topaz	Red Coral or Jasper	Yellow Sapphire or Yellow Topaz	Blue Sapphire or Lapis-Lazuli	Blue Sapphire or Lapis-Lazuli	Yellow Sapphire or Yellow Topaz
	RULING PLANET	Mars	Venus	Mercury	Moon	Sun	Mercury	Venus	Mars	Jupiter	Saturn	Saturn	Jupiter
GEMSTONE		Bloodstone	Turquoise	Peridot		Bloodstone	Peridot	Turquoise	Bloodstone	Citrine	Amethyst	Amethyst	Citrine

Different dates are shown for the Western or Tropical system of Astrology, and the Eastern or Sidereal system of Astrology. The reason is that the Western is based on the ecliptic, or Earth's orbit around the sun,* and the Eastern is based on fixed stars and constellations of stars outside this solar system, which were known to be in the exact same position thousands of years ago as they are today. We believe the Eastern system to be more accurate, but have provided both as reference.

*which changes slightly year to year

◈ PLANETARY JEWEL DESIGNS

© 1992 by Howard Beckman. All Rights Reserved.

126

THE SEVEN SECRETS OF SUCCESSFUL PROGRESS

These seven basic mental disciplines will help anyone to motivate themselves to attaining their maximum potentials in life. It is not enough that we have our charts done to understand our natural capabilities for success, as well as talents, in different areas. We must then discipline ourselves to develop the character and perseverance to fulfil our hopes and dreams. These disciplines or, once mastered, habits will help anyone to attain success to the maximum of their potential.

The first principle is POSITIVE THINKING. Negativity achieves nothing. We have to be positive and be willing to act properly, according to the dictates of our intelligence. Don't give in to being whimsical about your progress in life, whatever you are trying to accomplish. Look at difficulties as hurdles to be jumped on the way to your ultimate success. So-called failures should be seen as bringing success that much closer. Look at incompleteness as the "glass is always half-full", rather than the negative concept of the "glass being half-empty". People that adopt and maintain a positive attitude toward life not only have the greatest successes but obtain the greatest satisfaction from life in general. Try it and you'll see how much better you feel!

The second principle for success is to SET OUT YOUR GOALS IN LIFE. One of the most worthy disciplines is to take a pen and paper and write down the things you wish to accomplish in the coming year. Just list them, that's all. Then make a list of the things you'd like to accomplish in the next two years. Then list what goals you'd like to attain in the next three years, five years, ten years, and twenty years. Once you've done this, take a moment to think about what you've written and the goals which you've set down on paper. You'll find that there are many things you'd like to accomplish in life. Where do you see yourself next year, the year after, or in ten or twenty years?

Having this list will enable you to make intelligent plans to accomplish your aspirations in life. It is a fact that all successful people do this!! Once you have set out and defined the objectives you can begin to work toward their fulfilment, always keeping the goal in mind. Don't be someone that "can't see the forest for the trees". Keep the final objectives close to mind and heart and you will be able to muster the attitude, courage and perseverance to keep going until you fully realize your objective. Those that quit in mid-stream have forgotten the final objective, looking only at small pieces that may be causing temporary difficulty. Always remember the goal and you will get there eventually.

The third principle is TIME MANAGEMENT. Having defined the actions necessary to achieve the goal, you must then put them in the proper order. We are logical beings and if you take the time to plan, things will go much more smoothly and objectives will be reached, step by step. There are always so many small objectives within the big picture and, although we must always keep the total picture and ultimate goal in mind, we must also know which actions to perform and in what order, to build the consequence we desire from our work.

Be thorough in your evaluation of a situation and decide what little things must be done to accomplish the objective. Then start from the beginning. Do things step by step, not overlooking anything necessary to build yourself a strong foundation. A house is only as strong as its foundation so do things whereby each succeeding task will take you steadily toward the accomplishment of your objectives. "First things first" is a term used by others for this basic principle which I term "time management".

The fourth principle is CONSIDERATION, looking at each situation in which you deal with other people thoroughly and fairly. You must not only fulfil your own needs and objectives, but satisfy those of the people you intend to work with, or that may work for you. Everyone should be a winner, not someone a winner and someone a loser. To be a leader requires that you consider everyone and not selfishly consider only your own desires and needs. Find a way of arranging things so that everyone is felt to be of consequence. Good communication skills are a must!! Communication is 90% of everything we do. "No man is an island" is a very fitting saying in this regard. We need to be able to work with others and, in so doing, create a situation where we further ourselves toward the attainment of our objectives and present things so that others also feel that they are making positive gains toward their own objectives.

The fifth principle is LEARNING TO LISTEN. If you become a good listener, then you will understand what another is looking for and can come up with solutions to satisfy your mutual objectives. If you listen to others, really trying to understand them, (not thinking of what you are going to say next, while they're speaking) you will become well-liked and appreciated as a good manager. As a result, others will listen to you!

We all have basic similarities, yet there are also so many differences, for we are individuals. We have different karma, destinies and different ways of looking at things according to our perceptions of the world. This is beyond dispute. If we listen to others, considering what they have to say and their feelings, our powers of communication will be enhanced. When someone sees that you truly care enough to listen to them when they speak, they will not only listen to your viewpoint but be much more enthusiastic about your possible solution. Everyone wants to feel appreciated and if you empathise with others, then you will be listened to and be able to also get your own points across in a positive manner.

Naturally following, the sixth principle is COOPERATION, learning to co-operate with others and to instill in them the confidence to cooperate with you. Once you have utilized the principle of listening, you must learn how to put words into action. The actions must be cooperative so everyone involved feels that their actions are important to the achievement of the final objective. It doesn't matter what you're trying to do. There must be cooperation between all parties for results to be fully attained. Don't just listen to others (the fifth principle), yet fail to incorporate their feelings and ideas into the master plan. Give credit where credit is due. Many employees feel used and abused when their employers put across their ideas for something, yet fail to credit them with the work. Remember that everyone deserves respect and recognition for the good work that they do. Make a fully cooperative effort with those you work with and you will see enthusiasm and cooperation being reflected.

The seventh principle is to KEEP A BALANCE in life. One of my main platforms for complete, holistic and healthy life is maintaining good physical, mental and spiritual health, at all times. We cannot put too much effort into one without the other factors of our being suffering. Set yourself out a program for living a disciplined life for accomplishing all three of these objectives. Make a time for your spiritual meditation, prayer, worship or reflection. Keep that time sacred, for the most part, allowing only a real emergency to infringe upon it. We are not these bodies and at the time of death the only thing that goes with us is our spiritual advancement. In your next birth you will once again pick up from the point at which you left off at death in this lifetime. Everything else you build in life is finished- your material knowledge and accomplishments, your possessions and your familial relationships, so this effort is all-important for any sane person.

You must set aside the time to eat properly, to get adequate rest and to do some physical exercise. It's absolutely necessary if you wish to have a body that serves you well, even in old-age. It doesn't matter whether you exercise in the morning or evening, four days a week or seven days a week. We have different bodies that take different amounts of exercise to stay healthy and we have different likes and dislikes as to the activity performed for physical exercise. Set yourself a discipline in this regard and stick to it.

Then there is the mental and emotional health. You won't have lasting or fulfiling relationships with others, nor will you feel happiness or satisfaction, unless you are of good mental health. Develop positive character traits and don't give in to lower urges that lead to negativity. Show compassion and empathy toward others. Be an honest and straightforward person as much as possible. Don't put work ahead of everything so that your health suffers, or your spiritual side remains undeveloped. Many people in the West do this to the exclusion of all else. The results are always regrettable. Neglecting family causes its break-up. Neglecting health causes physical break-down. Not building good principles and character of the heart can lead to wrongful actions, which bring on distress and poor emotional development can also lead to mental nervous breakdowns. Remember to always rejuvenate yourself in these ways and you will maintain the ability to act for your own benefit, as well as others, throughout your life.

Mastering these seven principles takes care and dedication but doing so will make you someone that perseveres, achieves, is respected and, most importantly, is a contented, satisfied and happy individual. Desire success, think success, act utilizing these principles and you will be successful to the limits of your full potential. It is your birthright.

SAMPLE HOROSCOPE

Born at 18.00 on Saturday July 25, 1953 at Philadelphia, Pennsylvania U.S.A.
Latitude: 39° 57' North   Longitude: 75° 9' West
Local Sidereal Time 13:12:38 Greenwich Sidereal Time: 18:13:14 Time Zone: 05:00 DST: 01:00
Ayanamsa: 23° 12' 33"

Ascendant in	Sagittarius	4° 0'		
Sun in	Cancer	9° 16'		8th House
Moon in	Capricorn	1° 21'		2nd House
Mercury in	Cancer	11° 0'	Rx	8th House
Venus in	Taurus	27° 0'		6th House
Mars in	Cancer	5° 9'		8th House
Jupiter in	Taurus	24° 21'		6th House
Saturn in	Virgo	30° 0'		10th House
Rahu in	Capricorn	10° 0'	Rx	2nd House
Ketu in	Cancer	10° 0'	Rx	8th House

The Moon is full and waxing at 99°

4th Pisces	5th Aries	6th Taurus Venus 27° 0' Jupiter 24° 21'	7th Gemini
3rd Aquarius	Birth Chart for Sample Horoscope		8th Cancer Sun 9° 16' Mercury 11° 0' Mars 5° 9' Ketu 10° 0'
2nd Capricorn Moon 1° 21' Rahu 10° 0'			9th Leo
1st Sagittarius Ascendant 4° 0'	12th Scorpio	11th Libra	10th Virgo Saturn 30° 0'

11th Pisces	12th Aries Rahu	1st Taurus Ascendant	2nd Gemini
10th Aquarius	Navamsa Chart for Sample Horoscope		3rd Cancer
9th Capricorn Moon			4th Leo Venus Mars Jupiter
8th Sagittarius	7th Scorpio	6th Libra Ketu	5th Virgo Sun Mercury Saturn

3rd Pisces	4th Aries	5th Taurus Jupiter 27° 00′ Venus 24° 21′	6th Gemini
2nd Aquarius	Chandra Lagna for Sample Horoscope		Mars 5° 09′ Mercury 11° 00′ Sun 9° 16′ Ketu 10° 00′
1st Capricorn Moon 1° 21′ Rahu 10° 00′			8th Leo
12th Sagittarius	11th Scorpio	10th Libra	9th Virgo Saturn 30° 00′

DASA PERIODS FOR SAMPLE HOROSCOPE

Major	Minor	Period Begins	Major	Minor	Period Begins
Sun	Jupiter	from moment of birth	Saturn	Saturn	from June 16, 2008
Sun	Saturn	from April 23, 1954	Saturn	Mercury	from June 20, 2011
Sun	Mercury	from April 5, 1955	Saturn	Ketu	from February 27, 2014
Sun	Ketu	from February 9, 1956	Saturn	Venus	from April 8, 2015
Sun	Venus	from June 16, 1956	Saturn	Sun	from June 7, 2018
Moon	Moon	from June 16, 1957	Saturn	Moon	from May 20, 2019
Moon	Mars	from April 17, 1958	Saturn	Mars	from December 19, 2020
Moon	Rahu	from November 16, 1958	Saturn	Rahu	from January 27, 2022
Moon	Jupiter	from May 16, 1960	Saturn	Jupiter	from December 3, 2024
Moon	Saturn	from September 15, 1961	Mercury	Mercury	from June 17, 2027
Moon	Mercury	from April 17, 1963	Mercury	Ketu	from November 12, 2029
Moon	Ketu	from September 15, 1964	Mercury	Venus	from November 10, 2030
Moon	Venus	from April 16, 1965	Mercury	Sun	from September 9, 2033
Moon	Sun	from December 16, 1966	Mercury	Moon	from July 17, 2034
Mars	Mars	from June 17, 1967	Mercury	Mars	from December l6, 2035
Mars	Rahu	from November 13, 1967	Mercury	Rahu	from December 13, 2036
Mars	Jupiter	from November30, 1968	Mercury	Jupiter	from July 2, 2039
Mars	Saturn	from November 6, 1969	Mercury	Saturn	from October 7, 2041
Mars	Mercury	from December 16, 1970	Ketu	Ketu	from June 16, 2044
Mars	Ketu	from December 13, 1971	Ketu	Venus	from November 12, 2044
Mars	Venus	from May 10, 1972	Ketu	Sun	from January 12, 2046
Mars	Sun	from July 11, 1973	Ketu	Moon	from May 20, 2046
Mars	Moon	from November 15, 1973	Ketu	Mars	from December 19, 2046
Rahu	Rahu	from June 16, 1974	Ketu	Rahu	from May 17, 2047
Rahu	Jupiter	from February 27, 1977	Ketu	Jupiter	from June 4, 2048
Rahu	Saturn	from July 23, 1979	Ketu	Saturn	from May 11, 2049
Rahu	Mercury	from May 29, 1982	Ketu	Mercury	from June 19, 2050
Rahu	Ketu	from December 16, 1984	Venus	Venus	from June 17, 2051
Rahu	Venus	from January 3, 1986	Venus	Sun	from October 16, 2054
Rahu	Sun	from January 3, 1989	Venus	Moon	from October 16, 2055
Rahu	Moon	from November 28, 1989	Venus	Mars	from June 16, 2057
Rahu	Mars	from May 29, 1991	Venus	Rahu	from August 16, 2058
Jupiter	Jupiter	from June 16, 1992	Venus	Jupiter	from August 16, 2061
Jupiter	Saturn	from August 4, 1994	Venus	Saturn	from April 16, 2064
Jupiter	Mercury	from February 14, 1997	Venus	Mercury	from June 17, 2067
Jupiter	Ketu	from May 23, 1999	Venus	Ketu	from April 17, 2070
Jupiter	Venus	from April 28, 2000	Sun	Sun	from June 17, 2071
Jupiter	Sun	from December 28, 2002	Sun	Moon	from October 4, 2071
Jupiter	Moon	from October 16, 2003	Sun	Mars	from April 4, 2072
Jupiter	Mars	from February 14, 2005	Sun	Rahu	from August 10, 2072
Jupiter	Rahu	from January 21, 2006	Sun	Jupiter	through July 4, 2073

CONCLUSION

That astrology can be an extremely accurate and enlightening science when practiced by a qualified practitioner is known by all that are fortunate enough to have been introduced to it in a proper way. That it is so useful in understanding present and future faculties, opportunities and difficulties is not so astounding provided there is understanding of the natural laws of cause and effect operating within the universe. Through birth after birth, we are transmigrating from one body to another, through 8,400,000 species of life, from plant life to the aquatics, insects, animal kingdom and to the human form of life.

We are awarded a particular type of body according to our desires and the activities we perform once attaining the human form of life. There are basic similarities between human beings and the animals. We all eat, sleep, mate and fear for our defence of body and property. We humans make beautiful arrangements of our food, eating on tables with china, silverware, etc., whereas the animal just puts mouth directly to their food and eats. Ultimately there is no real difference. The food goes through the same processes to maintain the body. What is not burned as fuel is turned to stool and eliminated. Therefore, although we have a more polished way of acting during the ingestion of food, qualitatively there is no real difference.

We humans make soft beds and comfortable arrangements for our sleeping, whereas an animal lies down under a tree, in a cave or some such other place, to sleep. Still it is the same. We sleep, just as the animals do. What of mating, the ritual of sex? Animals do it, just as we do.

We go through so many elaborate rituals, preparations and psychological phantasmagoria for our love lives. We place the most concentration on this compared to any other category of material life, yet is it any different than the mating dances or rituals of the animals and other species of life? In reality it is qualitatively the same. We do it and they do it. A driving force sees to it that all species of life are procreated.

Lastly there is the "fearing" propensity, the desire to protect what is considered "personal property". The animals will protect their families, homes and mark out their territory, to ward off others. Anyone that has had a cat or dog as a pet can attest to this. The cat or dog marks their territory by urinating around the boundaries. Any other cat or dog that tries to infringe on their territory will generally be attacked forthwith. We humans constantly worry about our families, our bank accounts, acquiring more and defending what we have from others. We collect so much "stuff" that we actually become prisoners of our possessions. We must put burglar alarms in our cars and homes for fear someone will rob us. So much energy is wasted mentally and physically in the drive to acquire temporary things. There is no permanent value, for our very bodies are not permanent.

Animals are even more accomplished in these basic propensities than we humans are. An elephant can eat far more than the largest man or woman. A bear can sleep for months. A pigeon can have sex hundreds of times daily and the lion can swiftly defend and conquer more expertly than we can. Their bodies are suited to far greater enjoyment of these basic animal propensities and our own enjoyment of these things is actually less than theirs. Regardless of eating your favourite foods in a mannerly way, your enjoyment of them is no more than the enjoyment a pig experiences in eating fresh stool. It is a fact, however humourous this may sound! The pig relishes stool as its favourite food and will quickly gobble it up so that another doesn't try to steal even a morsel! The enjoyment we feel from sleep or sex is also no more than that experienced by the animals and probably less!

The real qualitative difference between human beings and the animal kingdom is the degree of intelligence and the ability to question our existence, to be self-conscious. We have the ability to ponder the questions of who am I? Who is God? How did I get here and where am I going? What are the duties of humans that are different from the animals? This is what sets us apart from the lower species of life. A person that pays no attention to answering these most important queries is verily living a life on a par with that of the animals.

We must always seek knowledge. I've heard people with no experience of astrology say they don't believe in it. I generally answer that your beliefs are based on emotions, not knowledge. One should always seek truth. The laws of the universe do not require man's sanction to operate. The law of gravity was in effect long before Newton "discovered" it, as were all the forces of nature before man assigned his own terms to them. What chaos would ensue if man's validation were needed!!

We must endeavour to answer these most important questions of life, progressing on the path towards self-realization. This is the duty of every person. This science of astrology gives us so much information about our past, present and future, while inhabiting these bodies. The more knowledge we have the easier it will be to succeed in all endeavours we engage in. I have tried to practically show how astrology can be relevant and of incalculable benefit in our daily lives in guiding ourselves, our families, etc. toward directions that will bring the greatest chance of success and satisfaction in life. If we use our horoscope as a guide we know better how and when to make decisions, the types of activities best suited to us and the times when different occurrences and situations will manifest. Why go through life haphazardly when such an awesome tool is available to enable us to willfully achieve success?

Ultimately, vedic astrology is meant to instigate our desire for self-realization. That the birth chart can give so much information is wonderful, yet what we are experiencing is a direct result of our actions in our last life. Therefore, we should be realizing that if I lived so many times before, then the idea of identifying with the body as the "self" is an absurdity. In this lifetime you may be called Tom, Raoul, Helen, Rajiv, Susan, etc., but that identity will be finished at the time of death, just as each identity you had in every previous birth was finished with the death of the body. Therefore we must come to the conclusion that we are not these bodies but our true "self" is that which inhabits the body, that force which gives life to the body. Without the presence of spirit soul, the body is but a lump of dead matter. The soul is what makes a person attractive. Regardless of how beautiful a woman's body may be, if spirit soul is not present no man has any attraction for the dead body. Is this not a fact?

These lives are fleeting and making plans to enjoy "permanency" in this world is foolishness. At the time of death, everything we have accomplished, gained, etc. in reference to the body and this lifetime, will be finished. You can take nothing with you, so of what value is spending so much of our valuable time engaged in those things meant only for annihilation in the near future? I am not suggesting that we fail to perform our duties to self, family, community, country, etc. These things are necessary, but we should always keep in mind that these things are not the goal of life. The real goal of human life is SELF REALIZATION THAT WILL ULTIMATELY LEAD TO GOD-REALIZATION. Only spiritual advancement will allow increased knowledge of your eternal nature in full joy and happiness. You must give great effort to investigation of the real problems of human life, namely birth, death, old age and disease. These problems cannot be solved through any material endeavour. We are cheating ourselves if we do not heed our inner call for spiritual knowledge, just as we cheat ourselves by not investigating the means to full attainment of our goals in this world.

The astrological horoscope will give a map to achieving success in all areas of life, physical, mental, emotional and spiritual. It will give the keys to unlocking many doors in this life......and the next, but still it is our action that shapes our destiny. We must have knowledge first of how, when and where to act but then it is up to each and every one of us to do so. To be successful requires dedication. There are no short-cuts to true success in life. We must develop character within our hearts, developing traits of goodness. We must be willing to act not only in the best interests of ourselves and families but in the self-interest of all living entities within this world. To do so requires knowledge. Knowledge is the torchlight which dissipates the darkness of ignorance. Those in knowledge fear nothing, not even death. Death is only the cessation of activities within this body. This process of travelling from one bodily situation to another is called "transmigration of the soul". Astrology is the science of understanding this. Once understanding exists there must be a call to action. We must act to insure our progress in the future birth and to progress toward the ultimate goal of liberation from material entanglement.

Those seeking to progress must make themselves qualified to understand transcendental subject matter by developing higher qualities of goodness, compassion, honesty, forbearance, tolerance, equanimity, etc. Only those with minds undisturbed by the bodily senses (tongue, stomach and genitals) can fully attain self-realization. It is not that everyone must become a swami, or priest, etc. The point is that we must start somewhere. Begin by looking at yourself objectively. Have you developed the qualities in yourself that you respect in others? That is actually the beginning of spiritual life. We need patience, kindness, compassion and an equanimity towards all others in this world. Then think about the magnanimous arrangement of God's creation......the inconceivable greatness of the creation of this world, as well as innumerable other worlds and universes. We can then realize how small and insignificant we actually are. When a person develops true humility it is possible to begin true spiritual practice.

Begin by reading about vedic philosophy, such as the incredibly enlightening "Bhagavad-Gita As It Is" by A.C. Bhaktivedanta Swami. There are other books by this great author, a bona-fide guru in the line of "bhakti-yoga", the yoga of love and devotion to God. The other books by this great sage such as "Coming Back... the science of reincarnation", "Easy Journey to Other Planets", or "The Science of Self-Realization" are extremely powerful for stimulating your spiritual thought processes. Another book which is easy reading and provides a glimpse into the life of a spiritual seeker is "Autobiography of a Yogi" by Paramahamsa Yogananda.

Then set aside a few minutes daily to begin some meditation. You can begin as simply as sitting comfortably, preferably in the quiet early-morning hours and, with your back straight, begin to breathe deeply. Inhale and exhale through your nose, keeping your mouth closed. Within a minute you will feel a calmness begin to come over you. Relax your mind and try not to think about any of your daily activities, worries, etc. Softly, but loud enough for you to hear, repeat a mantra such as "Om Madhavaya Namaha" or "Om Govindaya Namaha". These are powerful mantras from the "Vishnu Sahastranam" or "Thousand Names of Vishnu". You will feel the sound vibration washing over your entire being to the depth of your consciousness. It will stimulate your remembrance of your spiritual self from many past lives and, in so doing bring a calmness and freedom from anxiety previously unknown. I will give guidance for more advanced practice of meditation in future books.

Remember that we cannot understand such advanced subject matter with our limited perception in this world, any more than a member of an African tribe who had never seen people outside of their jungle village could understand our Western existence. Were you able to take one member of the village away in a box and drop him in the middle of London, removing the box, he would be stunned. The dearth of his knowledge acquired in the rural village in Africa would be of almost no use to understanding this city with its bustling traffic, buildings, people's lifestyles, etc. There would be total bewilderment and great fear, due to a lack of knowledge of the environment.

By the same token, we cannot understand what life is like on other planets in this universe by our experience of life on earth, what to speak of other universes, in this vast material manifestation. Most especially, we cannot perceive of life beyond the material stratosphere or of an eternal existence beyond it, by our experience or knowledge of material activities. We must look for an authority, a basis for understanding. If you didn't know who your father was, the only bona-fide authority would be your mother. Her answer would be authoritative. Similarly the vedas are considered to be the authority for the human race to gain knowledge in all areas of life but most especially for knowledge of our true, eternal, constitutional position as spirit and how to gain realization of this. That is the most important engagement of a human being, man, woman, or child. We must learn how to keep spiritual health just as we learn how to keep physical health. Nothing is of greater importance.

I would urge anyone desiring a tool for achieving full potentials in life to have their chart done by a qualified vedic astrologer. Then so many questions we all have about our thinking, feeling and mental processes can be answered. We can also fully understand ourselves, how we got here and how we can act to achieve the most happiness and satisfaction. This is your birthright, as it is the birthright of everyone.

It is my sincere hope that this text may serve as a beginning for many to investigate the wealth of knowledge contained within the vedas and that it may help to reinstate vedic astrology as a most valuable life tool in the minds of the populace in the West.

Anyone wishing to contact the author Howard Beckman about attending lectures, workshops and seminars on vedic astrology, or to arrange full-life horoscope, or other astrological services, may contact us at our address in England, or the U.S.

**6 White Rock Gardens
Hastings, E. Sussex TN34 1LD
England, U.K.**

**1601 One Independence Place
Philadelphia,
Pennsylvania
19106
U.S.A.**